THE MOORISH CONQUEST

800 Years of Moorish Rule

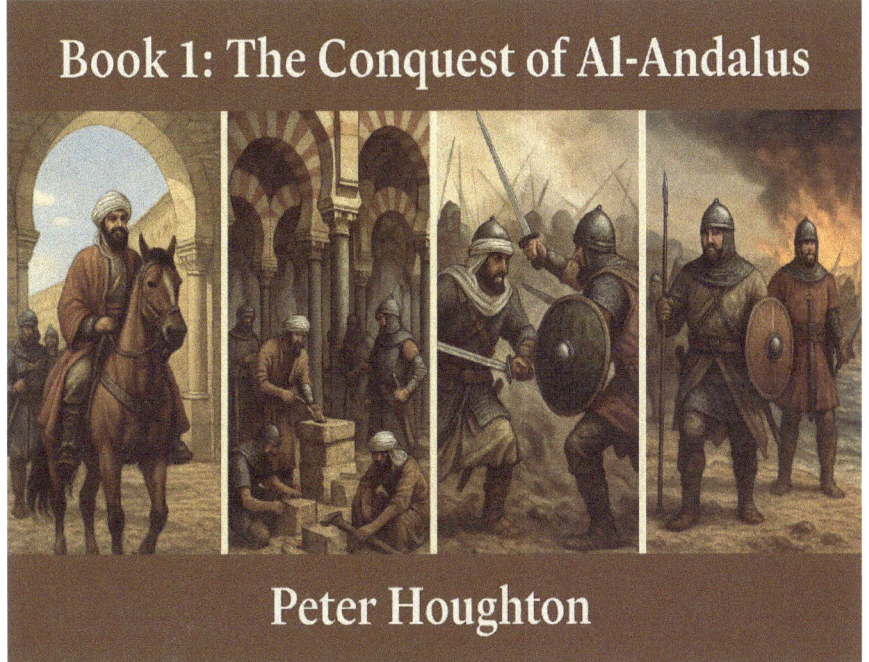

© Copyright 2025 Peter Houghton. All rights reserved.

It is illegal to reproduce, duplicate or transmit any part of this document in either electronic means or printed format. Recording of this publication is strictly prohibited.

Acknowledgments

This book — The Fall of Al-Andalus — began not simply as a story, but as an act of remembrance. To write of the final centuries of Muslim Spain is to enter a world of faith, ambition, tragedy, and transformation; a world where empires rose and fell, yet human courage endured.

Many hands, voices, and hearts helped bring this work to life. I owe a profound debt of gratitude to the historians and scholars whose painstaking research illuminated the lost landscapes of medieval Iberia — the chroniclers of Córdoba and Granada, the translators of Arabic archives, and the modern historians who continue to recover the echoes of that vanished civilisation. Their scholarship turned fragments into a narrative, and from their dedication I drew both accuracy and inspiration.

To those who walk the streets of Spain with an eye for its hidden history — the travellers, photographers, and teachers who see more than stones and ruins — thank you. Each city still whispers fragments of the past: the call to prayer that once drifted over Seville, the arches of Córdoba that still hold their light, the fortress walls of Granada that remember everything. Your passion kept those echoes alive in my imagination.

To my colleagues and readers who followed this journey from the beginning, I offer sincere thanks for your patience, encouragement, and curiosity. The discussions that began as brief exchanges grew into reflections on empire, faith, and humanity. You reminded me that history is not merely written — it is shared, questioned, and lived again through those who care to understand it.

To my family and friends who endured endless conversations about kings, caliphs, and crusaders, your support gave this project its quiet strength. To those who encouraged me during the long hours of research and rewriting — when ancient maps and chronicles blurred into nights without end — your belief made the difference between abandonment and completion.

I also wish to acknowledge those who lived the history we now study — the nameless chroniclers, artisans, scholars, and ordinary people who witnessed the splendour and sorrow of Al-Andalus. This book is, in part, their voice — a remembrance of what was built, what was lost, and what survived in spirit when the banners fell.

And finally, to the people of Spain — heirs to a land that has known many faiths, tongues, and empires — this book is written in recognition of your layered heritage. The story of Al-Andalus is not one of division, but of coexistence and transformation. It belongs to all who walk these landscapes today, where Moorish fountains still flow beside Christian spires, and the shadows of history still mingle with the light of renewal.

To all who have kept the memory of Al-Andalus alive — scholars, poets, and dreamers — may this work stand as both tribute and continuation.

The Fall of Al-Andalus was born from reverence for the past and belief in the enduring capacity of the human spirit to rebuild, remember, and rise again.

Dedication

I would like to dedicate these books to my family,

to my darling wife, Jolanta, who is my rock,

My calm in the storms, and my best friend.

United, we are stronger.

For your patience, love, and unwavering belief.

For the quiet hours you allowed these pages to be written,

for every shared story, memory, and encouragement along the way.

This journey, though written in ink, was built upon your support.

To my sons, Daniel, Dominic, and Luke,

who have brought such joy and pride into our lives,

and to their partners, Katie and Vanessa,

whose warmth and support have enriched our family even more.

And to my wonderful grandchildren,

whose laughter keeps me young and whose curiosity reminds me

why stories—both real and imagined—matter.

They have all been the quiet strength behind every page,

the constant source of love, inspiration, and purpose.

These books may bear my name, but they carry our story within them.

And to a very special person called Bill,

who has been, and continues to be,

a fantastic help in creating these books and the many to come.

His guidance, creativity, and persistence

have been invaluable in bringing these works to life.

This journey would not have been possible without him.

It is safe to say that Bill is truly unique.

There is nobody else quite like him.

About The Author

Peter Houghton was born in Barnet, Hertfordshire, in 1955 and moved to Falmouth in 1966. He attended Wellington Terrace Junior School and later Trescobeas School, leaving in 1971.

His career began at Choaks Bakery, where he worked until 1976. He then joined Louis Patisserie in Hampstead, where he met his future wife. In 1985, the couple opened their own bakery business in Wooburn Green, later relocating to Romford, where they successfully ran a new bakery until 2005.

That year, Peter sold the business and moved to Spain to become Sales Director for a Spanish developer, overseeing the UK and Irish markets. The 2009 financial crisis brought that chapter to a close. After a brief retirement, he became actively involved in local politics.

In 2017, he joined a local political party and helped it develop into a voice for the coast. After leaving the party in 2018, he co-founded a new political movement advocating for the independence of Orihuela Costa, a reflection of his deep commitment to the community and his belief in fair representation for coastal residents.

In 2023, Peter was successfully elected by the residents of Orihuela Costa to serve on the Government District Board for Orihuela Costa.

Author's Note

Why I Am Creating the Moorish Conquest

History is often presented as a procession of kings and battles, a sequence of dates that conceals more than it reveals. The Moorish Conquest seeks to restore depth and texture to medieval Iberia by telling its story slowly, honestly, and with a human scale.

Across these volumes, I follow the long arc from the Visigothic twilight to the rise of Al-Andalus, its splendour, fractures, and eventual fall—not as myth, but as lived experience. I am drawn to the moments where power turns on quiet decisions: a midnight council, a negotiated surrender, a frontier pact that saves a village and reshapes a kingdom.

This series is written to honour complexity: the coexistence and conflict of Muslims, Christians, and Jews; the rivalries of courts and clans; the resilience of ordinary people navigating empires. By moving era by era, I aim to let each century breathe, allowing readers to feel the weight of time, the contingency of events, and the humanity within the chronicles.

Modern Spain carries deep echoes of its past—in institutions, in habits of power, in the recurring struggle between reform and inertia. Shadows Over Spain is my attempt to trace those structures with clarity and moral seriousness: to examine how corruption takes root, how trust erodes, how accountability is built—or evaded—and how citizens push back.

These books are not merely narratives of scandal; they are studies of systems: the law, finance, media, and the everyday decisions that accumulate into culture. I aim to connect episodes to their causes, and policy to lived reality, so that readers can see not just what happened, but why—and what might be done differently.

Series Dedication

To those whose voices echo across centuries;

To the historians, storytellers, and anonymous chroniclers who preserved the memory of a land where faiths met, armies clashed, and civilisations intertwined;

To the men and women of Al-Andalus—Muslim, Christian, and Jewish—who lived through triumph and tragedy, whose lives shaped the destiny of a peninsula and the identity of a continent;

And to all those who walk the ruins, read the chronicles, and still hear the whispers of Córdoba, Granada, and Toledo in the stones;

To the people of Al-Andalus… to those who once called its gardens home, who built its mosques and libraries, who spoke in the music of Arabic, Latin, and Castilian,

This book is dedicated to your memory.

To every artisan, scholar, and farmer who endured the tides of conquest and faith yet left behind a trace of beauty, this is written in your honour;

And to the people of Spain today, heirs to a land woven from many histories, may you never forget that the soil beneath your feet once nurtured coexistence as well as conflict, wisdom as well as war,

May the echoes of Al-Andalus remind us all that the past, however fractured, still calls us toward understanding.

Contents

Prologue – The Crossing 1
Preface 10
Series Introduction 12
Chapter Highlights 14
⚔ Chapter 1 ⚔ The Fall of the Visigoths: A Kingdom of Fissures 18
    The Dual Society: A Roman Core, A Gothic Shell 18
    A Flawed Crown: The Perils of the Elective Monarchy 19
    Religious Tensions: The Crisis of the Jewish Community 21
    The Rise of Roderic and the Final Fracture 22
    Aftermath 25
⚔ Chapter 2 ⚔ The Crossing and the Fall of a Kingdom 26
    The Hammer Blow 26
    The Night Crossing: The Razor's Edge 27
    The Myth and the Resolve 28
    The Pre-Battle Manoeuvres: King in the North 28
    Guadalete – The Decisive Battle (July 711) 29
    The Treachery and the Vanishing 31
    The Road to Conquest: Mūsā's Arrival 32
    The Final Prize: Toledo 33
    The End of Visigothic Rule: The Birth of Al-Andalus 33
    Aftermath 35
⚔ Chapter 3 ⚔ The Burden of Victory 36

The Tragedy of the Conquerors: Mūsā and Ṭāriq 36
The Administrative Tether: Kairouan and Córdoba 38
Pragmatic Coexistence: The Dhimma System 38
The Great Divide: Arab and Berber Rivalries 39
The Push North and the Fixed Frontier 40
The Halt at Tours (Poitiers) 41
A Province Both Promising and Precarious 42
Aftermath 44

⚜ Chapter 4 ⚜ The Flight of the Falcon: ʿAbd al-Raḥmān I and the Birth of Independence 45
The Fugitive Prince: A Dual Heritage 45
Six Years in the Wilderness: The Making of a Leader 46
The Maghreb Crossroads and the Hope of Al-Andalus 47
Al-Andalus: Ripe for the Pluck 47
The Crossing and the Call to Arms 48
The Battle of the Masāra and the Seizure of Power 49
The Emirate Founded: A Calculated Sovereignty 50
Aftermath 53

⚜ Chapter 5 ⚜ Forging a New Dynasty: The Falcon of Quraysh 54
I. The Umayyad Refugee and the Scars of Al-Andalus 55
External Threats 55
II. Centralisation: The Emir's Pragmatic Hand 56
Retribution and Administration 57
Infrastructure and Cultural Legacy 57

Reshaping Córdoba 57

The Great Mosque as Ideological Statement 58

Conclusion: Setting the Pattern 58

Aftermath 60

⚸ Chapter 6 ⚸ A Century of Struggle: Consolidation, Crisis, and the Dawn of Culture 61

I. Hishām I (788–796): Piety, Law, Lingering Tensions 61

II. Al-Ḥakam I (796–822): The Test of Central Authority 62

The Toledo Revolt (805) 62

Internal Purge 63

Abd al-Raḥmān II (822–852): The Zenith of the Emirate 63

Economic Transformation 64

The Blossoming of Córdoba 64

Recurring Unrest and the Unshaken Emirate 65

External Pressure 66

Aftermath 67

⚸ Chapter 7 ⚸ The Stones of Power and the Golden Age: Architecture, Infrastructure, and Renaissance 68

The Great Mosque: An Architectural Declaration of Sovereignty 69

Erasure of the Visigoths (The Past) 70

The Evolution of Style and Synthesis 70

The Mosque as Political and Spiritual Anchor 70

Strategic Investment in Infrastructure and Defence 71

The Northern Thughūr (Frontiers) 71

The Agricultural Revolution: The Waters of Prosperity 72

Economic Flow and the Cultural Renaissance.......................... 72

Commerce and Global Reach 73

Attracting the Ahl al-'Ilm (People of Knowledge) 73

Aftermath 75

✼ Chapter 8 ✼ Faith and Power: The Social Fabric of Al-Andalus
.... 76

The Structure of Religious Coexistence: The Dhimmi System 76

Rights and Protections 77

The Price of Protection: Taxes and Subordination................... 77

The Internal Dynamics of Muslim Society 78

The Problem of the Muwalladūn 79

The Vital Role of Jewish and Christian Communities............. 79

The Jewish Contribution 79

The Mozarabic Community 80

The Legacy of Convivencia 80

Aftermath 82

✼ Chapter 9 ✼ The Crisis of the 9th Century: The Anatomy of Collapse.. 83

The Roots of Disintegration... 83

Political Impotence and Fiscal Drain 84

The Rebel's Genesis and Base 85

From Bandit to Sovereign.. 85

The Extent of the Crisis 86
Aftermath 88

※ Chapter 10 ※ The Road to Unity: ʿAbd al-Raḥmān III and the Reassertion of State Power 89

The Policy of Absolute Submission... 89
Swift and Relentless Campaigns.. 90
The Fall of Bobastro 90
Reasserting Authority on the Frontiers 91
The Chain of Defence 91
Administrative and Military Reform 92
Dismantling the Old Guard.. 92
The Professional Army of Loyalty... 92
Aftermath 94

※ Chapter 11 ※ The Dawn of the Caliphate: The Ultimate Declaration of Sovereignty 95

The Political Imperative: Claiming the Successorship 95
The Decline of the Abbasids (The East) 96
The Threat of the Fatimids (The South) 96
The Transformation of Sovereignty 97
The New Regnal Identity 97
Consolidating Legitimacy at Home 97
International Diplomacy and Mediterranean Influence 98
Aftermath 100

✘ Chapter 12 ✘ City of Light: The Splendour of Caliphal Córdoba
.... 101

I. Architecture: Symbols of Global Authority 101

II. Economic and Urban Sophistication 103

III. The Intellectual Beacon 104

IV. The Management of Diversity and Security 105

Aftermath 107

✘ Chapter 13 ✘ Blood at the Borders: Warfare and the Frontier Life
.... 108

I. The Nature of the Thughūr 108

II. The Rhythm of Border Warfare 109

III. Caliphal Response and the Paradox of Trade 111

Aftermath 113

✘ Chapter 14 ✘ The Holy Road: Arteries of Power and Piety ... 115

I. Strategic Design and Scope 115

II. The Trinity of Function: Faith, Force, and Finance 116

III. A Microcosm of Andalusi Society 118

Aftermath 119

✘ Chapter 15 ✘ The Last Campaign of Ibn Marwān: Asserting Caliphal Reach 120

The Legacy of Western Autonomy 120

The Muwallad Stronghold 120

The Strategic Imperative 121

Al-Ḥakam II's Campaign: Force and Prudence 122

The Siege of Marvão 122

The Aftermath and Legacy 123

Aftermath 125

⚔ Chapter 16 ⚔ The Threshold of Greatness: Zenith and the Seeds of Decline 126

The Zenith of Córdoba: A City Unmatched 126

The Fragility of Personal Rule 127

Aftermath 131

⚔ Chapter 17 ⚔ The Clash at Tours 134

Historical Reflection 142

Strategic Withdrawal 144

Frankish Triumph and Legend-Making 145

A Frontier Redrawn 146

The Long Shadow of Tours 147

Aftermath 149

Epilogue to the Chapter 151

⚔ Bonus Chapter ⚔ Between Two Dawns: The Last Council of Toledo 152

Historical Reflection 161

Epilogue Moment 162

Epilogue – The Gathering Storm 162

Glossary of Key Terms 166

Prologue – The Crossing

The year 711 was not so much a beginning as an eruption long prepared. On moonless nights, the Strait of Gibraltar is a narrow, breathing thing, the black water folding and unfolding between two coasts that almost touch.

Fishermen knew its moods; pilots measured its tides by the tilt of starlight; smugglers swore the current itself whispered secrets in Arabic one hour and in Latin the next. Across it came a small army, scarcely twelve thousand, most of them Berbers newly folded into Islam, led by a frontier general whose name would claim the rock itself: Ṭāriq ibn Ziyād.

Later chroniclers swore he burned his ships to harden his men. Whether the flames were wood or legend, the message was iron. There would be no easy road back. No safe compromise with the far shore.

They had not been sent to plant a new world; they were dispatched to exploit the rot in an old one. The Visigothic kingdom in Iberia—Christian in confession, Roman in habits, Germanic in pedigree—had split along a jagged seam. King Roderic had taken the throne amid accusations of usurpation, while the circle around the late King Witiza sharpened their knives in exile and intrigue.

From Ifrīqiya, Mūsā ibn Nuṣayr, governor and sober accountant of opportunity, weighed the reports: an elective crown that invited conspiracy, overmighty nobles with private levies, bishops divided by policy and pride, Jewish communities ground down by law and longing for reprieve, and cities accustomed to bargaining for their lives. He allowed the probe.

Ṭāriq came ashore on a tooth of stone the Arabs would call Jabal Ṭāriq—Gibraltar. The landing was not triumphal. Men waded, coughing brine, hauling bundles of grain, spare tack, and the iron heads of spears. Scouts were sent to test the paths inland; guides were paid in coin and promises. In the first days, the army looked less like a conquering host than a disciplined caravan that had accidentally brought too many swords.

The first serious answer came from Roderic himself, riding south with a host patched together from feudal obligation and fear. They met near the Guadalete in the furnace of high summer.

What happened on that field will be argued so long as men argue: which wing buckled, which noble held back, whether treachery turned the line. The meaning, however, is not disputed. Roderic fell. The last claim to unified Visigothic authority fell with him.

What followed was not simply a storm of swords. It was a cascade of negotiations. Seville looked over its walls, counted its food, weighed the risk, and opened its gates under terms. Toledo, ancient heart of Gothic rule, bargained hard, then yielded without a sack.

Those who surrendered paid jizya or kharāj; those who resisted learned the harsher arithmetic of siege. New governors were appointed; qāḍīs took their seats beside notaries who still wrote in Latin; tax rolls were copied; oaths were sworn. Arabic words began to settle over old streets like a second skin.

The conquerors named the land al-Andalus and sent letters eastward heavy with numbers: grain tallies, tribute, lists of horses and hostages—the vocabulary by which distant caliphs understood far provinces.

Speed disguised fragility. Arab commanders and Berber captains brought with them older rivalries; the roads ran longer than the lash could reach; the Strait was a temperamental messenger.

The push beyond the Pyrenees, bold and briefly successful, met a Frankish counterblow at Tours in 732 that taught limits without undoing what Iberia had become. In the north, mountain enclaves of Christians learned endurance and the geometry of the pass. In the south, the new rulers learned that holding a land is slower work than taking it.

Yet even in those first decades, there were signs of a different fate. The soil answered new waterworks with surplus; terraces stitched green into brown hillsides; markets swelled with saffron, indigo, and silk braided to local wool and wine.

The old Roman towns found a fresh rhythm under the call to prayer. In ledgers and harvests and the slow, patient copying of books, a frontier began to imagine itself as a centre.

Then, in 750, the eastern centre tore itself apart. The Abbasids rose on a tide of blood and calculation, and Umayyad princes were cut down at a table laid for reconciliation.

One young survivor slipped the net: ʿAbd al-Raḥmān ibn Muʿāwiya, a prince on the run with Berber kin to hide him and a memory of rule to steady him. He threaded the Maghreb like a hunted falcon and turned his eyes to the peninsula where the sea ends and the rivers begin. If Ṭāriq's crossing had opened a door, ʿAbd al-Raḥmān meant to build a house on the threshold.

Al-Andalus was not born in a day, nor solely in battle. It emerged from bargains under city gates and arguments in council halls, from aqueducts and orchards and the grammar of taxes, from tolerances measured in law and limits enforced by garrisons.

It began as a wound in one kingdom and a frontier in another, and became, in time, its own centre of gravity—a place where a fallen dynasty would plant its standard and where Europe would learn to read its own future in Arabic script.

The year 711 was not so much a beginning as an eruption long prepared. On moonless nights, the Strait of Gibraltar is a narrow, breathing thing, the unfolding between two coasts that almost touch.

Fishermen knew its moods; pilots measured its tides by the tilt of starlight; smugglers swore the current itself whispered secrets in Arabic one hour and in Latin the next.

Across it came a small army, scarcely twelve thousand, most of them Berbers newly folded into Islam, led by a frontier general whose name would claim the rock itself: Ṭāriq ibn Ziyād.

Later chroniclers swore he burned his ships to harden his men. Whether the flames were wood or legend, the message was iron. There would be no easy road back. No safe compromise with the far shore.

They had not been sent to plant a new world; they were dispatched to exploit the rot in an old one. The Visigothic kingdom in Iberia—Christian in confession, Roman in habits, Germanic in pedigree—had split along a jagged seam. King Roderic had taken the throne amid accusations of usurpation, while the circle around the late King Witiza sharpened their knives in exile and intrigue.

From Ifriqiya, Mūsā ibn Nuṣayr, governor and sober accountant of opportunity, weighed the reports: an elective crown that invited conspiracy, overmighty nobles with private levies, bishops divided by policy and pride, Jewish communities ground down by law and longing for reprieve, and cities accustomed to bargaining for their lives. He allowed the probe.

Ṭāriq came ashore on a tooth of stone the Arabs would call Jabal Ṭāriq—Gibraltar. The landing was not triumphal. Men waded, coughing brine, hauling bundles of grain, spare tack, and the iron heads of spears. Scouts were sent to test the paths inland; guides were paid in coin and promises. In the first days, the army looked less like a conquering host than a disciplined caravan that had accidentally brought too many swords.

The first serious answer came from Roderic himself, riding south with a host patched together from feudal obligation and fear. They met near the Guadalete in the furnace of high summer.

What happened on that field will be argued so long as men argue: which wing buckled, which noble held back, whether treachery turned the line. The meaning, however, is not disputed. Roderic fell. The last claim to unified Visigothic authority fell with him.

What followed was not simply a storm of swords. It was a cascade of negotiations. Seville looked over its walls, counted its food, weighed the risk, and opened its gates under terms. Toledo, ancient heart of Gothic rule, bargained hard, then yielded without a sack.

Those who surrendered paid jizya or kharāj; those who resisted learned the harsher arithmetic of siege. New governors were appointed; qāḍīs took their seats beside notaries who still wrote in Latin; tax rolls were copied; oaths were sworn. Arabic words began to settle over old streets like a second skin. The conquerors named the land al-Andalus and sent letters eastward heavy with numbers: grain tallies, tribute, lists of horses and hostages—the vocabulary by which distant caliphs understood far provinces.

Speed disguised fragility. Arab commanders and Berber captains brought with them older rivalries; the roads ran longer than the lash could reach; the Strait was a temperamental messenger. The push beyond the Pyrenees, bold and brief.

Successful, met a Frankish counterblow at Tours in 732 that taught limits without undoing what Iberia had become. In the north, mountain enclaves of Christians learned endurance and the geometry of the pass. In the south, the new rulers learned that holding a land is slower work than taking it.

Yet even in those first decades, there were signs of a different fate. The soil answered new waterworks with surplus; terraces stitched green into brown hillsides; markets swelled with saffron, indigo, and silk braided to local wool and wine. The old Roman towns found a fresh rhythm under the call to prayer. In ledgers and harvests and the slow, patient copying of books, a frontier began to imagine itself as a centre.

Then, in 750, the eastern centre tore itself apart. The Abbasids rose on a tide of blood and calculation, and Umayyad princes were cut down at a table laid for reconciliation. One young survivor slipped the net: ʿAbd al-Raḥmān ibn Muʿāwiya, a prince on the run with Berber kin to hide him and a memory of rule to steady him.

He threaded the Maghreb like a hunted falcon and turned his eyes to the peninsula where the sea ends and the rivers begin. If Ṭāriq's crossing had opened a door, ʿAbd al-Raḥmān meant to build a house on the threshold.

Al-Andalus was not born in a day, nor solely in battle. It emerged from bargains under city gates and arguments in council halls, from aqueducts and orchards and the grammar of taxes, from tolerances measured in law and limits enforced by garrisons. It began as a wound in one kingdom and a frontier in another, and became, in time, its own centre of gravity—a place where a fallen dynasty would plant its standard and where Europe would learn to read its own future in Arabic script.

Preface

The history of Al-Andalus is more than the story of conquest and collapse. It is the story of encounter—between cultures, between empires, and between visions of the world.

For nearly eight centuries, the lands of Iberia were a crossroads of civilisations, a place where power shifted like desert sands and identities were forged and contested in equal measure.

Yet the story of Al-Andalus is too often told in fragments: a battle here, a caliph there, a single dazzling century of culture or a single dramatic fall.

This series, The Moorish Conquest, was born from a desire to tell that story as a journey, not a footnote. Each book follows a thread in the vast tapestry: from the first crossing of Tariq ibn Ziyad's armies to the slow, painful twilight of Muslim rule in Granada.

The focus is not solely on kings and conquerors, but on the shifting structures of society, the resilience of communities, and the human cost of empire.

This revised edition of Book 1: The Fall of Al-Andalus expands upon that original vision.

Chapters have been refined, historical contexts deepened, and the narrative reshaped to better illuminate the forces that made Al-Andalus both a beacon of brilliance and a battleground of ambitions.

It is not a simple tale. It is a chronicle of splintered loyalties, faith and pragmatism, shifting alliances, and unexpected consequences. And like all chronicles, it is both a mirror to the past and a quiet echo of the present.

Series Introduction

The Moorish Conquest unfold over multiple volumes, tracing the rise, splendour, and eventual fall of Muslim Iberia. Each book builds upon the previous, following the evolving political, cultural, and military landscape of the peninsula:

Book I – The Fall of Al-Andalus

The Visigothic world collapses before the sudden surge of Tariq ibn Ziyad's armies. Toledo falls not by siege, but by fracture. A new order begins.

Book II – The Crescent Rises

Power consolidates. Córdoba emerges as the beating heart of a new civilisation, and the Emirate takes shape amid rivalry and revolt.

Book III – The Caliphate Ascendant

Al-Andalus becomes a cultural and political powerhouse under Abd al-Rahman III and al-Ḥakam II—until cracks begin to show beneath the splendour.

Book IV – Fractured Crescent

Internal divisions, Berber revolts, and shifting frontiers fracture the once-mighty Caliphate, paving the way for taifa rivalries.

Book V – The Last Kingdom of Al-Andalus

Granada stands alone—a brilliant, fragile court under the shadow of advancing Christian kingdoms.

Each book is meticulously researched, blending narrative clarity with historical fidelity. Together, they offer a panoramic view of one of the most complex and transformative periods in European history.

Chapter Highlights

1. The Fall of the Visigoths: A Kingdom of Fissures

On the eve of the Muslim invasion, internal divisions fracture the Visigothic kingdom. Nobles feud, bishops jockey for influence, and cracks appear that will soon become fatal breaks.

2. The Crossing and the Fall of a Kingdom

Tariq ibn Ziyad's daring crossing from North Africa in 711 brought swift collapse to Visigothic power. Guadalete becomes the turning point that opens Iberia to a new era.

3. The Burden of Victory

Rapid conquest brings both triumph and strain. Armies spread thin, alliances fray, and the challenges of administering a vast new land quickly emerge.

4. The Flight of the Falcon: ʿAbd al-Raḥmān I and the Birth of Independence

Fleeing the Abbasid massacre, a young Umayyad prince crosses to Iberia. His survival and ambition will change the fate of Al-Andalus.

5. Forging a New Dynasty: The Falcon of Quraysh

'Abd al-Raḥmān I consolidated his power through force and diplomacy, establishing Córdoba as the seat of a new, independent emirate.

6. A Century of Struggle: Consolidation, Crisis, and the Dawn of Culture

The young emirate faces rebellions, rivalries, and frontier threats while laying the foundations of governance and cultural development.

7. The Stones of Power and the Golden Age: Architecture, Infrastructure, and Renaissance

Córdoba rises as a monumental city. Mosques, palaces, aqueducts, and roads reflect both political power and cultural ambition.

8. Faith and Power: The Social Fabric of Al-Andalus

Muslims, Christians, and Jews coexist uneasily under Islamic rule. Taxes, privileges, and tensions define a complex, layered society.

9. The Crisis of the 9th Century: The Anatomy of Collapse

Rebellions, fiscal strain, and regional separatism bring the emirate to the brink of fragmentation, as rivals like 'Umar ibn Ḥafṣūn challenge Córdoba's authority.

10. The Road to Unity: 'Abd al-Raḥmān III and the Reassertion of State Power

A young ruler with iron resolve restores central authority through relentless campaigns and administrative reform.

11. The Dawn of the Caliphate: The Ultimate Declaration of Sovereignty

In 929, ʿAbd al-Raḥmān III proclaims himself Caliph, elevating Córdoba to a rival of Baghdad and Mahdia, and reshaping the Mediterranean balance.

12. City of Light: The Splendour of Caliphal Córdoba

At its zenith, Córdoba dazzles the world with its architecture, libraries, commerce, and Convivencia — a beacon of urban sophistication.

13. Blood at the Borders: Warfare and the Frontier Life

Along the thughūr, soldiers, settlers, and raiders live in a harsh borderland where the Battle of Simancas exposes both power and vulnerability.

14. The Holy Road: Arteries of Power and Piety

Roads and watchtowers bind Al-Andalus together, blending pilgrimage, trade, and military control into a single network of authority.

15. The Last Campaign of Ibn Marwān: Asserting Caliphal Reach

Al-Ḥakam II moves west to crush the last vestiges of autonomy, bringing the Marwānid domain under full Caliphal control.

16. The Threshold of Greatness: Zenith and the Seeds of Decline

The golden age peaks under al-Ḥakam II, but power quietly shifts to Almanzor, sowing the seeds of future fracture.

17. The Clash at Tours

Across the Pyrenees, ʿAbd al-Raḥmān al-Ghāfiqī meets Charles Martel in a legendary confrontation between cavalry and infantry, ambition and endurance.

Bonus Chapter — Between Two Dawns: The Last Council of Toledo

A reflective look at the twilight of Visigothic power and the dawn of a new era, where memory and myth converge on the threshold of transformation.

⚔ Chapter 1 ⚔
The Fall of the Visigoths: A Kingdom of Fissures

By the dawn of the 8th century, the Iberian Peninsula was a kingdom in name but a political, economic, and social battlefield in practice.

The Visigoths—a Germanic people who had settled after crossing from Gaul in the early 5th century—had ruled for nearly three hundred years. They had replaced the fading Western Roman Empire as the dominant political force, yet they had never truly replaced it in spirit or foundation.

The Dual Society: A Roman Core, A Gothic Shell

The Visigothic regime was an unstable political layer imposed upon a deep-seated Hispano-Roman foundation. Most of the population, estimated conservatively between five to seven million people, remained Hispano-Roman. The Visigoths themselves were a small, insular military and aristocratic elite, perhaps constituting only 5% to 10% of the total population.

• Cultural Continuity: Latin remained the language of sophisticated administration, law, and high culture. Roman infrastructure—the vast network of roads, aqueducts, and municipal organisation in major cities like Toledo, Mérida, Seville, and Zaragoza—continued to function.

The Visigothic monarchs ruled primarily through Roman structures, a testament to the enduring power of imperial bureaucracy.

The Land Divide: This duality created a profound economic chasm. The Visigothic warrior elite and the Church controlled massive, often tax-exempt latifundia (estates).

Most of the populace—Hispano-Roman peasants, serfs, and free farmers—laboured under crippling burdens of taxation, arbitrary military levies, and legal restrictions enforced by an elite whose political loyalty was often questionable. The wealth of the kingdom was concentrated among a few hundred widespread resentments.

This social structure gave the kingdom a strong appearance but fatal fragility. They had achieved religious unity under Catholicism with the conversion of King Reccared I in 587 CE, but they had utterly failed to achieve social or political cohesion.

A Flawed Crown: The Perils of the Elective Monarchy

The greatest structural weakness of the Visigothic state was its elective monarchy—a system engineered for perpetual chaos.

Kings were chosen from among the leading noble families by a council of powerful nobles and bishops, often formalised in the Councils of Toledo.

In theory, this ensured that the most capable leader commanded the realm. In practice, it meant that every royal death triggered a civil war.

Succession by Bloodshed: Few kings in the last century of the kingdom died peacefully. Assassination was not the exception but a common feature of succession.

The councils that met to proclaim the new ruler were often preceded by bloody purges, backroom bribery, and the execution or exile of the losing faction.

A new king always began his reign politically and psychologically isolated, wary of the very men—the Dukes and Counts—who had just elevated him.

The Rise of Warlords: The instability at the top bred widespread decentralisation. Ambitious nobles maintained vast, private armies (exercitus privatus) and heavily fortified estates, ready to defy royal authority, refuse tax collection, or switch allegiance when the inevitable political crisis erupted.

The political loyalty of the kingdom was fragmented into dozens of armed noble retinues, not a unified royal army.

The Church's Power: The Church, though a unifying force of doctrine, was equally a player in these intrigues. Bishops controlled immense wealth and often held the decisive swing vote in Toledo, entangling religious power in messy, often lethal, court politics.

The central state was thus little more than a fragile alliance of convenience.

Religious Tensions: The Crisis of the Jewish Community

The religious unity of the kingdom under Catholicism came at a high cost, creating a vast, disaffected internal minority: the Jewish communities of Iberia.

These communities, concentrated in the economic centres of Toledo, Córdoba, Mérida, and Seville, were crucial to the kingdom's economy as traders, financiers, and specialised craftsmen.

Yet, their importance was overshadowed by religious and political pressure from the powerful, often fanatical, episcopacy.

Fluctuating Tolerance: Their status violently fluctuated between periods of economic valuation and systematic persecution.

Systematic Persecution: By the 7th century, under the decrees of the Councils of Toledo, policies swung toward outright oppression. Laws forbade the practice of the Jewish faith, mandated the confiscation of property, and often enforced baptism under threat of exile.

The Final Acts: Under King Egica (687–702), the anti-Jewish measures reached a peak, culminating in forced conversions, the seizure of Jewish-owned land, and even the enslavement of Jewish children—a move designed to eliminate the community through cultural extinction.

By 710, these communities had no loyalty to the Visigothic crown.

For them, the arrival of a new, potentially tolerant, Muslim regime was a calculated risk that offered a significant improvement over the existential threat posed by the ruling Christian monarchs.

Their neutrality, and later their cooperation in garrisoning conquered cities, would prove vital to the invaders' rapid success.

The Rise of Roderic and the Final Fracture

In 710 CE, the fatal climax of the Visigothic structural flaws arrived. The throne was seized by Roderic (Rodrigo), a seasoned dux (military commander) from the southwest. His accession was illegitimate and deeply contested.

Roderic had likely usurped the throne following the death of his predecessor, King Witiza, effectively seizing the crown from Witiza's young sons and brothers.

This created the powerful and armed Witizan party, which viewed Roderic as a tyrant and usurper.

The Witizan Exile: Rather than accept quiet exile, the Witizan faction retreated to the southern provinces, particularly Baetica, fortifying themselves and plotting revenge. Crucially, some took refuge in the strategic fortress of Ceuta, across the Strait of Gibraltar, which was garrisoned by Berber troops under the authority of the governor of Ifrīqiya, Mūsā ibn Nuṣayr.

The Fatal Invitation: This was the irreversible fracture. The exiles sent envoys across the Strait to Mūsā, offering a cynical alliance: ships, intelligence, and troops to help overthrow Roderic. They sought a political coup; they inadvertently triggered a conquest.

The military structure was equally fractured. The Visigoths did not maintain a large, unified professional army.

Kings relied on the feudal obligation of nobles to raise troops. When Roderic finally raised an army to counter the invasion, it was a fragmented, reluctant collection of private retinues, loyal more to their regional lords than to their despised king.

By contrast, the invading force of Ṭāriq ibn Ziyād—approximately 7,000 to 12,000 men—was unified, professional, and hardened by continuous campaigns.

Roderic, preoccupied with a separate campaign in the north against Basque rebels, left the critical southern coast dangerously exposed. His absence gave Ṭāriq and Mūsā the perfect moment to act.

The kingdom on the brink was about to be pushed over the edge. The invasion of 711 was not the beginning of the kingdom's fall— it was merely the sound of the structure finally collapsing under its own immense internal strain.

For decades, the Visigothic realm had been a mosaic of fragile loyalties rather than a unified nation. Kings rose and fell not by succession, but by conspiracy. Noble factions schemed endlessly within the crumbling palaces of Toledo, their ambitions outpacing their capacity for governance. The once-mighty church, now entangled with aristocratic privilege, offered divine sanction to whichever faction briefly seized the throne. Beneath that veneer of sanctity, the countryside was restless — its peasants overtaxed, its provincial governors half-independent, its border defences neglected.

The assassination of King Witiza and the disputed accession of Roderic had split the realm in two. To the north, rival nobles plotted his downfall; to the south, exiled factions invited foreign intervention, seeking vengeance cloaked in piety. It was a civil war masquerading as politics, and when the Berber and Arab forces landed across the straits at Gibraltar, they did not find a kingdom ready to repel them. They found one already exhausted, its armies divided, its treasury looted by years of factional greed.

The Visigothic court mistook the invasion for a mere raid — a border nuisance like many before it. Yet within months, the banners of Islam advanced inland, moving not as conquerors but as opportunists following the scent of decay. The fall of the Visigoths was not a sudden cataclysm; it was a slow unravelling, centuries in the making, brought to its violent conclusion by a single, decisive gust from across the sea.

Aftermath

The crossing of Tariq ibn Ziyad and his army in 711 did more than open a new military campaign; it fundamentally altered the trajectory of Iberian history. The invasion shattered the assumption that the peninsula's geographical barriers—the Strait of Gibraltar and the Pyrenees—were enough to keep the outside world at bay.

The speed and confidence with which the Muslim forces landed reflected a broader transformation in Mediterranean power dynamics. The Islamic caliphate had, within a century, expanded from Arabia to North Africa, creating a political, cultural, and economic sphere that was both dynamic and ambitious. Iberia was not an isolated conquest; it was part of a global civilizational surge that connected Damascus, Cairo, Kairouan, and eventually Córdoba.

The landing also marked the beginning of a centuries-long process of cultural layering. Unlike many previous invasions, the Muslim armies brought not just swords but administrators, merchants, jurists, and scholars. Their aim was not simply to raid, but to govern and reshape. This set the stage for a complex society that would soon blend Islamic governance with local Visigothic and Hispano-Roman traditions.

The invasion's psychological impact was immense. Within a single generation, what had been a distant, almost unimaginable threat became a lived reality for the peoples of Iberia. Towns and cities accustomed to Christian Visigothic rule now faced entirely new rulers with different languages, religions, and legal systems. It was the beginning of a new epoch—not a passing storm.

⚔ Chapter 2 ⚔
The Crossing and the Fall of a Kingdom

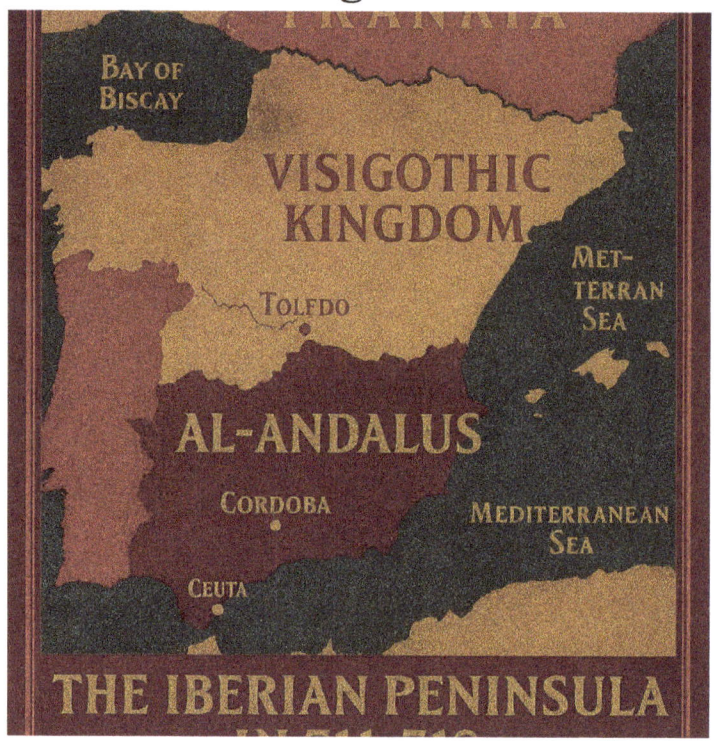

The Hammer Blow

The spring of 711 CE marked the decisive, irreversible moment for Iberia. The invasion force, assembled on the North African coast near Ceuta, was not a massive army of occupation, but a specialised, lightning-fast strike team.

Their Numbers were around 12,000 men—a figure slightly larger than the initial scouting force—it was a precise blend of experienced Arab commanders providing cavalry and high command, and tenacious Berber tribesmen forming the bulk of the swift infantry and light horse.

Many were recent converts to Islam, bringing with them the fierce discipline and endurance of the Maghrebi mountains and deserts.

Their leader, Ṭāriq ibn Ziyād, was a Berber freedman and client of Mūsā ibn Nuṣayr. A man of modest, non-aristocratic birth, his authority rested entirely on his exceptional military skill and absolute loyalty. Mūsā had chosen him precisely because he was bold, adaptable, and unafraid of risking everything—qualities lacking in the stagnant Visigothic nobility.

The Night Crossing: The Razor's Edge

The Strait of Gibraltar is narrow—only thirteen kilometres at its shortest point—but it was a dangerous frontier patrolled intermittently by Visigothic or Byzantine vessels.

Ṭāriq's crossing, launched in April 711, was not a grand armada; it was a carefully choreographed series of small, swift voyages utilising merchant transports, fishing boats, and ships allegedly provided by the disgruntled Count Julian.

Logistical Stealth: The transports hugged the waves, relying on the darkness of the moonless nights and the shifting currents to avoid detection.

The psychological pressure on the troops was immense; the strait was known for sudden storms, and a single Visigothic patrol could have easily scattered the vulnerable vessels.

Jabal Ṭāriq: The landing was secured on the monumental, rocky promontory that would forever bear his name: Jabal Ṭāriq (the Mountain of Ṭāriq), later Anglicised to Gibraltar.

This choice was strategic: The Rock was easily defensible, providing a secure beachhead and observation point.

The Myth and the Resolve

Later chroniclers would weave the dramatic tale that Ṭāriq ordered his ships to be burned upon landing to eliminate any possibility of retreat. While likely a powerful piece of propaganda, the sentiment was undoubtedly true: for the 12,000 invaders, there was no easy retreat across the turbulent strait.

Their only path lay forward, into the sprawling, internally fractured kingdom of the Visigoths.

The Pre-Battle Manoeuvres: King in the North

Fortune continued to favour the invaders with devastating precision. News reached Ṭāriq that King Roderic was not near the southern coast, but far in the north, suppressing a rebellion by Basque tribes.

His army was consequently dispersed across the peninsula, and he would need crucial weeks, if not months, to consolidate the feudal levies and march south.

Ṭāriq seized the initiative. He immediately pressed inland, executing a brilliant pre-emptive campaign in the southwestern region known as Baetica.

His light, mobile Berber forces struck quickly, avoiding large fortifications but seizing key river fords, outposts, and roads leading toward the capital, Seville.

This forced a confrontation before Roderic could gather his strength, isolating the Visigothic garrisons and demoralising the local nobility.

Roderic, upon receiving the alarming news, abandoned his northern campaign. He began a desperate, hurried march south, sending urgent summons to his often-disloyal nobles.

He needed to defend the heartland, but he was forced to fight on the enemy's terms, with a cobbled-together army.

Guadalete – The Decisive Battle (July 711)

The two armies finally met in midsummer 711 near the river Guadalete (or perhaps the nearby river Barbate, in an area often referred to as Lake La Janda.

The engagement was less a battle between equals and more a demonstration of the internal corrosion of the Visigothic state.

Roderic's Host: Roderic's host, though potentially numbering 25,000-40,000 men—significantly outnumbering Ṭāriq's force—was a precarious patchwork. It consisted of levies from different regions, troops loyal to the King, and crucially, formations commanded by the deeply resentful Witizan nobles.

Roderic may have even donned an extravagant chariot and purple robes, attempting to project an image of imperial majesty that his political situation utterly belied.

The Feline Focus: Ṭāriq's troops fought as a unified whole, their morale high, fighting for conquest and spoils. The battle lines were drawn. The disciplined, swift Arab cavalry focused its charge on the flanks, attempting to bypass the heavy, cumbersome Visigothic infantry.

The Berber infantry pressed relentlessly in the centre, their light armour giving them superior mobility in the summer heat.

The Treachery and the Vanishing

The decisive factor, according to both Arab and later Christian chronicles, was betrayal and defection.

The forces commanded by the Witizan nobles—the very faction that had invited Mūsā to intervene—held back or openly switched sides mid-battle, leaving Roderic's centre exposed and his flanks in chaos.

Whether this was a calculated defection or merely a withdrawal born of deep political resentment, the effect was devastating.

By day's end, Roderic's army was in full rout.

The psychological and military backbone of the kingdom was broken. King Roderic himself vanished from the battlefield. Some chroniclers claimed he drowned in the muddy river, weighed down by his regal armour; others suggested he fled.

Whatever the truth, his disappearance—a profound symbolic failure—shattered what little unity and legitimacy remained in the Visigothic state. The royal seal was broken, and the heart of the resistance was gone.

The Road to Conquest: Mūsā's Arrival

The victory at Guadalete changed the entire trajectory of the campaign. What had begun as a mere raid or a coup attempt instantly became a full-scale conquest.

Ṭāriq advanced rapidly, using the Hispano-Roman roads and targeting the administrative and economic centres.

Towns fell with startling speed.

Settlements and Surrender: The vast majority of towns did not resist. Cities like Écija and later Córdoba were quickly taken, often after brief sieges or negotiation.

Surrender was typically exchanged for guarantees of life, property, and religious freedom, allowing local Christian and Jewish communities to continue their lives, though under the terms of dhimma, or tribute (the jizya tax).

The Governor's Advance: In June 712, Mūsā ibn Nuṣayr himself arrived with a fresh, much larger contingent of Arab elite troops and seasoned North African generals, bringing the total Muslim force to perhaps 18,000–20,000. Mūsā was reportedly jealous of Ṭāriq's spectacular, rapid success and immediately began his own line of conquest further west.

Working separately, Mūsā secured the crucial western provinces, taking Seville (which held out longer than most) and the ancient

Roman city of Mérida after a protracted and difficult year-long siege. Ṭāriq continued his march, focusing on the central plains.

The Final Prize: Toledo

The jewel came in 714, when Toledo, the Visigothic capital, opened its gates after negotiation. The city had been abandoned by its nobles and its archbishop, who fled north, taking what was left of the royal treasury and the religious relics.

The local population, including the substantial Jewish community, offered no resistance. The speed of the collapse astonished both conqueror and conquered. In less than three years, the political structure of a three-century-old kingdom was obliterated.

The End of Visigothic Rule: The Birth of Al-Andalus

By 718, Muslim control stretched across most of the peninsula, from Gibraltar in the south to the Ebro Valley in the northeast. The Visigothic kingdom had ceased to exist as a political entity.

The conquest was not a total ethnic cleansing. It was a rapid political and military takeover facilitated by internal corruption and division. The land had not been simply defeated; it had been replaced,

Often, with the tacit consent of the local population, who exchanged a fractured, oppressive Christian elite for a unified, disciplined, and initially more tolerant Muslim administration.

The new rulers called the land Al-Andalus—a name likely derived from the Roman Vandalicia or perhaps simply the land of the West.

They intended not merely to hold it, but to make it their own, establishing a frontier of faith and culture that would shape European history for the next eight centuries.

Often, with the tacit consent of the local population, who exchanged a fractured, oppressive Christian elite for a unified, disciplined, and initially more tolerant Muslim administration. The new rulers called the land *Al-Andalus*—a name likely derived from the Roman *Vandalicia* or perhaps simply "the land of the West."
They intended not merely to hold it, but to make it their own, establishing a frontier of faith and culture that would shape European history for the next eight centuries.

For many Iberians, the change was less a conquest than a reordering. The Muslim governors arrived with an unexpected pragmatism: they retained much of the existing taxation system, respected property rights, and allowed local Christian and Jewish communities to maintain their laws and faiths under the *dhimma* system. To the peasantry, weary of noble exactions and ecclesiastical tithe, this was not subjugation but a reprieve — the replacement of chaos with efficiency, and of distant oppression with immediate order.

Yet the transformation was far deeper than political. Within a generation, new cities flourished, trade routes reopened, and Arabic replaced Latin as the language of administration.

Aftermath

The Visigothic collapse after Guadalete revealed a kingdom that had been politically brittle long before the first Muslim horseman set foot in Iberia. Succession crises, aristocratic rivalries, and the weakening of royal authority left the Visigothic elite unable to mount a coordinated defence.

The defeat was not merely military; it was ideological and psychological. The monarchy had projected an image of divine sanction and continuity with Roman authority. The speed of its unravelling broke that illusion. For many local elites, submission to the new rulers was preferable to chaos or civil war.

This vacuum of authority allowed the Muslim forces to consolidate control with startling efficiency. Instead of encountering unified resistance, they found fragmented local power structures willing to negotiate. The fall of the Visigoths, therefore, cannot be understood simply as a military conquest—it was also a political absorption of a failing state.

In the long run, the memory of this collapse would shape Christian resistance ideology. Pelayo's rebellion in Asturias, for example, was not merely about local survival; it was framed as the restoration of a lost Christian order—a memory weaponised for centuries to come.

⚔ Chapter 3 ⚔
The Burden of Victory

By the year 718 CE, scarcely seven years after the first crossing at Gibraltar, the banners of Islam flew from the windswept cliffs of the Atlantic coast to the shadowed foothills of the Pyrenees.

The astonishing speed of the conquest—which secured approximately 80% of the Iberian Peninsula—had stunned friend and foe alike. But military triumph, as history often proves, carries its own immense burdens. The real work—far slower, more delicate, and fraught with unseen political and ethnic dangers—was only beginning.

The Tragedy of the Conquerors: Mūsā and Ṭāriq

The immediate consequence of their dazzling success was the downfall of the two men who had orchestrated it.

Mūsā ibn Nuṣayr and Ṭāriq ibn Ziyād, the architects of this breathtaking expansion, had delivered unimaginable riches to the Umayyad Caliph, al-Walīd I, in Damascus. Reports spoke of gold plates from Visigothic treasuries, rare silks and spices captured in Andalusi ports, and legions of prisoners whose ransom would fund further campaigns.

Yet, the Caliph grew deeply suspicious of Mūsā's independent streak and the sheer scale of the treasure amassed. In a classic imperial move to curb potential rivals, Mūsā and Ṭāriq were both recalled to Damascus in 714 CE.

Public Humiliation: Mūsā was forced to parade his immense spoils through the streets of Damascus, showcasing his wealth before it was confiscated. He was publicly humiliated and died in relative disgrace.

The Fate of Ṭāriq: Ṭāriq, the former freedman, fared even worse. He was imprisoned and stripped of all command, fading quickly into historical obscurity—a clear warning to any provincial commander who achieved too much glory.

The abrupt departure of the two strong men left a profound political vacuum in Al-Andalus.

The rapid appointment of a series of short-lived governors (or walīs) highlighted the instability inherent in ruling a distant, newly conquered land.

The Administrative Tether: Kairouan and Córdoba

Al-Andalus, as the new rulers named the peninsula, was attached administratively to the governor of Ifriqiya (modern Tunisia/eastern Algeria), headquartered at Kairouan. This structure placed the province at the end of a long, fragile chain of command.

In practice, each link in the chain weakened the next. Orders from Damascus could take three to six months to reach Córdoba, making the governor's office (or walī) a powerful, semi-autonomous post.

In the interim, walīs acted according to circumstance, opportunity, and, often, personal ambition, frequently resulting in short, violent terms of office. Over the next four decades, Al-Andalus would see twenty-three different governors, a clear sign of chronic instability.

Pragmatic Coexistence: The Dhimma System

Early administration was brutally pragmatic. The Muslim rulers lacked the manpower to govern or farm the entire peninsula. They relied heavily on the existing social structure to maintain order and, crucially, to collect revenue.

Visigothic Aristocracy: Visigothic nobles who had surrendered on favourable terms often retained their estates and continued to oversee local tax collection under the new Muslim administration.

This kept local expertise in place and guaranteed revenue but created a patchwork of Christian autonomy within the Muslim order.

Cities and Taxes: Cities like Toledo, Seville, and Mérida that had opened their gates without a fight were granted protection treaties (pactos de capitulación). They were allowed to keep their churches, bishops, and self-governing councils, provided they paid two principal taxes promptly: 1. Jizya: A per-capita tax levied on non-Muslim men (the dhimmī).

Kharaj: A land tax levied on the vast estates, irrespective of the owner's religion.

This arrangement preserved stability, but the patchwork governance laid the groundwork for future revolts, as Christian lords retained significant regional power.

The Great Divide: Arab and Berber Rivalries

Beneath the veneer of Umayyad loyalty, the seeds of ethnic conflict—a conflict that would define the next century of Al-Andalus—were sown in the very distribution of the spoils. Old rivalries between Arab and Berber tribes, which had merely been suppressed by the unifying force of conquest, re-emerged with fierce territoriality.

Arab Privilege: Arab commanders, primarily from Syria (the Caliph's own power base) and Yemen (ancient Arab tribes), expected and received the richest lands: the fertile Guadalquivir river valley (al-Gharb), the established towns of Córdoba and Seville, and the most important administrative posts.

They settled in a semi-aristocratic style, importing Arab cultural and political norms.

Berber Marginalisation: The Berber troops, whose numerical strength (up to 70% of the initial forces) and ferocity had carried the day at Guadalete, were rewarded with grants in the less hospitable regions: the rocky, central Meseta, the isolated mountain passes, and the semi-arid lands of the south-east.

These lands were often colder, less productive, and perpetually exposed to Christian raiding.

Resentment festered, leading to mass desertions and, eventually, open revolts. The Berbers felt they had done the hard work of conquest only to be relegated to the periphery—a dangerous demographic bomb waiting to explode.

The Push North and the Fixed Frontier

The appetite for expansion was not sated by the conquest of Iberia. The Muslim advance surged northward beyond the Pyrenees into

Gaul, establishing a major, fortified foothold at Narbonne (Arbūna) in 720 CE. For a time, it seemed possible that the same wave that had overwhelmed Iberia might wash deep into Frankish territory.

The walīs saw Gaul as a continuous source of plunder and prestige. Successive governors, notably Al-Samh ibn Mālik al-Khawlānī, launched ambitious raids. The pinnacle of this advance was reached under 'Abd al-Raḥmān al-Ghāfiqī in 732 CE.

The Halt at Tours (Poitiers)

The advance reached its high-water mark in October 732, when the Muslim forces, laden with spoils from raids on Aquitaine, met the Frankish army led by Charles Martel (Charles the Hammer) between Tours and Poitiers.

The Battle of Tours (or Poitiers) was not catastrophic for the Muslims—they retreated mostly intact—but it was decisively strategic.

Fixing the Limit: The defeat fixed the northern limits of Al-Andalus along the Pyrenees. It proved that the logistical chain extending from Córdoba was too fragile and the Frankish resistance too disciplined for further large-scale, permanent settlement.

The Thughūr (The Marches): The frontier settled along the Pyrenees and the valleys beyond, defined by three fortified military districts known as the Marches (al-Thughūr).

Thughūr al-Aqsā (The Farthest March): Centred on Pamplona (later lost).

Thughūr al-Wusṭā (The Middle March): Cantered on Zaragoza.

Thughūr al-Adnā (The Nearest March): Centred on Barcelona (later lost).

This zone became both shield and sword—a defensive barrier against Christian incursions (the nascent kingdoms of Asturias, Navarre, and the Catalan counties), and a constant launch point for raids (ṣā'ifa) that kept the northern Christian kingdoms perpetually destabilised.

The Thughūr required continuous, expensive military deployment, particularly of the marginalised Berber troops.

A Province Both Promising and Precarious

By the mid-8th century, Al-Andalus was a prize and a problem in equal measure.

Its markets thrived with goods from Africa, the Middle East, and Europe; its fields, benefiting from new irrigation techniques, promised wealth beyond the wildest dreams of its first conquerors.

Yet beneath the surface, tensions brewed into a volatile mix:

1. Ethnic Rivalries: The disenfranchisement of the Berbers.

2. Geographical Challenge: The challenge of governing across the sea from Kairouan and Damascus.

3. Political Fragility: The uneasy partnership between conquerors and the still-powerful Christian landed aristocracy.

It was in this climate—a province both promising and precarious, on the verge of its own internal explosion—that a fugitive prince from the shattered heart of the Umayyad world would seek his salvation, and in doing so, transform Al-Andalus from a distant, restive outpost into an independent, sophisticated realm.

Aftermath

The rapid Muslim advance northwards demonstrated the adaptability of the early conquerors. Rather than rely solely on overwhelming numbers, they integrated diplomacy, strategic treaties, and targeted force. Many towns capitulated in exchange for protection, religious freedom, and tax agreements, creating a patchwork of arrangements that extended Moorish control far beyond the range of their initial armies.

This swift expansion changed the peninsula's demographic and cultural composition within years. Arabic and Berber settlers established garrisons and communities in key cities. New administrative divisions were overlaid on old Roman and Visigothic frameworks, gradually reshaping governance and land ownership patterns.

However, the very speed of expansion contained the seeds of future instability. Peripheral territories were lightly held, dependent on negotiated loyalties rather than entrenched institutions. As Christian enclaves in the north regrouped, these frontier zones would become the fault lines of centuries of conflict.

⚔ Chapter 4 ⚔
The Flight of the Falcon: ʿAbd al-Raḥmān I and the Birth of Independence

The year 750 CE brought an earthquake to the Islamic world. The venerable Umayyad Caliphate, which had reigned supreme from Damascus for nearly a century and directed the conquest of Iberia, was violently overthrown by the Abbasid Revolution.

Led by a coalition of aggrieved non-Arab converts (mawalī), Shi'a factions, and disenchanted Arab tribes from the eastern provinces, the revolution was brutally efficient. Members of the ruling Umayyad family were hunted down with relentless precision; entire branches of the dynasty were extinguished in a single night.

The most infamous of these purges—the "Dinner of Blood"—saw eighty Umayyad princes and officials massacred under the guise of reconciliation, ensuring that the former ruling house was extinguished forever.

The Fugitive Prince: A Dual Heritage

From this apocalyptic massacre, one man escaped to carry the torch of the dynasty. ʿAbd al-Raḥmān ibn Muʿāwiya, barely in his twenties, was a prince of both Arab and Berber blood. His father had been a Umayyad noble of Damascus; his mother, a Berber woman from the Nafza tribe.

This dual heritage was his salvation. It gave him not only a legitimate claim to the throne in the eyes of any loyal Umayyad Arab veteran but also a network of potential allies among the Berber tribes of North Africa—the very groups who often felt marginalised by the Arab elite.

Six Years in the Wilderness: The Making of a Leader

His flight was a legendary saga—a crucible that forged the young, privileged prince into a hardened, ruthless survivor and statesman. For six years (750–755 CE), he moved through the vast, hostile landscapes of the Near East and North Africa, relentlessly pursued by Abbasid agents whose orders were clear: leave no Umayyad alive.

The apprenticeship: ʿAbd al-Raḥmān learned the essential skills of command during this terrifying period of exile. He learned to travel light, to sleep in the saddles of fast horses, to judge men instantly, and to exploit local rivalries. He had to buy shelter with gifts one day and vanish before dawn the next.

Near Captures: His resilience became legendary. Twice, he narrowly avoided capture: once, fleeing from an Abbasid scouting party, he plunged into a frigid river, hiding in a well until his pursuers passed over; another time, he slipped away disguised as a common camel driver just as agents descended on his hiding place.

He was living history, dodging certain death through sheer will and cunning.

Loyalist Nucleus: As he traversed the Maghreb, his charisma and lineage began to draw men to him. He gradually gathered a small band of loyalists—former Umayyad retainers, tribal allies, and men who saw in him the chance to settle old scores against the new Abbasid regime. This small nucleus of devoted followers formed the core of his future government.

The Maghreb Crossroads and the Hope of Al-Andalus

The Maghreb itself was no haven. The region was still recovering from the devastating Great Berber Revolt of the previous decade, which had severely destabilised Umayyad control.

Arab governors in Ifriqiya eyed the fugitive prince with immense suspicion, seeing him as a political liability or a dangerous rival.

By 755 CE, ʿAbd al-Raḥmān realised his life depended not on finding safety in Africa, but on seizing power in a territory that was strategically vital yet politically chaotic: Al-Andalus.

Al-Andalus: Ripe for the Pluck

The province across the Strait was a picture of institutional decay, perfectly ripe for his ambition:

1. Ethnic Schism: The Arab and Berber factions quarrelled openly, often descending into outright civil war over land distribution and power.

2. Weak Central Authority: Governors (walīs) ruled like independent princes, refusing to cooperate or recognise external authority.

3. The Nominal Ruler: The current walī, Yusuf al-Fihri, held power tenuously by balancing rivalries but commanded little genuine loyalty from the dispersed, warring garrisons.

Al-Andalus desperately needed a figure who could unite its warring elements under a banner that was both legitimate (Umayyad lineage) and strong (military skill). ʿAbd al-Raḥmān, with his Arab-Berber blood and his dramatic escape story, was the perfect symbol.

The Crossing and the Call to Arms

In August 755 CE, ʿAbd al-Raḥmān, having arranged a secret passage, crossed the Strait. He landed on the Andalusi coast near Almuñécar.

His campaign was a masterclass in swift political mobilisation. He did not arrive with an invading army, but with an irresistible symbol: the last surviving prince of the fallen dynasty.

The Syrian Contingent: His first move was to appeal directly to the thousands of Syrian troops settled in the peninsula. These soldiers, remnants of the jund (military districts) established after the conquest, held deep loyalty to the Umayyad house, which had favoured them with land and prestige.

Under Yusuf al-Fihri's weak rule, their status had declined, fueling their resentment.

The Promise of Restoration: ʿAbd al-Raḥmān promised these Syrians the restoration of their former status and privileges. This core of seasoned, loyal Umayyad veterans immediately secured his military base. He secured their allegiance and began his march inland, his small force swelling with disaffected soldiers and opportunistic Berber allies.

The Battle of the Masāra and the Seizure of Power

The confrontation with Yusuf al-Fihri was swift, brutal, and utterly decisive. The armies met in March 756 CE near the banks of the Guadalquivir River, just outside Córdoba, in a clash known as the Battle of the Masāra (or the Battle of Musārah).

Yusuf's forces, composed of disparate local levies and Andalusi contingents, were poorly coordinated. ʿAbd al-Raḥmān's troops, though fewer in number, were cohesive, highly motivated by dynastic loyalty, and commanded with a singular purpose.

The young prince personally directed his disciplined Syrian force, routing the governor's army.

Yusuf al-Fihri fled, attempting to continue a rebellion on the margins before being cornered and executed shortly thereafter.

In May 756 CE, barely nine months after his clandestine landing, ʿAbd al-Raḥmān entered Córdoba as its undisputed ruler.

The Emirate Founded: A Calculated Sovereignty

ʿAbd al-Raḥmān's first act was one of strategic restraint. He did not claim the title of Caliph (Khalīfat Allāh)—the Commander of the Faithful—which was now claimed by the victorious Abbasids in Baghdad. That title would wait for another, stronger generation.

Instead, he proclaimed himself Amīr (Emir) of Córdoba, sovereign in all but name. This was a calculated choice: by avoiding direct challenge to the Abbasids' religious supremacy, he reduced the immediate and existential threat of their massive military intervention, even as he built a state entirely free of their political control.

The Falcon of Quraysh, as later poets would call him, had achieved the improbable: from hunted exile to founding sovereign.

Under his decisive hand, Al-Andalus ceased to be a remote, chaotic province of a far-off empire and became instead an independent Umayyad realm—the only surviving branch of a dynasty thought extinct.

It was a transformation that would shape the destiny of Iberia for centuries, setting the stage for an era of splendour, rivalry, and cultural flowering unmatched in the West. But it was also the beginning of new challenges, for to forge a dynasty was one thing; to keep the newly united, fragile emirate whole against internal dissent and northern hostility would be quite another.

The *Falcon* fled south through a kingdom in ruins. Every fortress passed was either abandoned or in enemy hands, every village a silent witness to the shifting of empires. The air itself seemed heavy with endings — the fall of kings, the death of languages, the slow fading of an old world that had ruled for three centuries. Yet amid the devastation, the young survivor carried something the invaders could not seize: the idea of continuity, of a lineage and a faith not yet extinguished. The road to survival was narrow, but it led toward promise — across deserts, seas, and centuries.

When ʿAbd al-Raḥmān finally reached al-Andalus, it was as though the winds had reversed. From fugitive to founder, from hunted prince to architect of a new civilisation, his flight became the seed of the Umayyad revival in the West. In Córdoba, he would raise not only walls and palaces but an idea — that exile could become empire, that the displaced could become the builders of destiny.

His arrival marked the transformation of al-Andalus from a conquered province into a beacon of Islamic power, intellect, and resilience. The flight of one man became the salvation of a dynasty — and the birth of a legend that would outlast the empire that chased him.

Aftermath

The failure to advance further after the Battle of Tours marked a strategic turning point. While often mythologised as a clash between Islam and Christendom, the battle's real significance lay in its redefinition of Moorish ambitions.

The defeat forced the rulers of Al-Andalus to shift from rapid imperial expansion to consolidation. It signalled that the push into Gaul had reached its natural logistical and political limits. Instead of looking northward for conquest, Córdoba began to turn inward, focusing on administration, integration of diverse peoples, and cultural development.

The encounter also shaped Frankish identity. Charles Martel's victory was elevated into legend, laying the foundations for Carolingian power and the idea of a Christian bulwark. For both sides, Tours became less a military episode and more a civilizational symbol—a narrative turning point that would echo for centuries.

The flight of ʿAbd al-Raḥmān was more than a tale of survival; it was the pivot upon which the fate of al-Andalus turned. From the blood-soaked sands of the Abbasid purge emerged not merely a refugee, but the architect of a new polity — a man who would transplant the memory of Damascus into Iberian soil and infuse it with Western vitality. His escape demonstrated that the empire was not a geography but an idea — one that could be reborn wherever vision and will endure. In the wake of his arrival, Córdoba ceased to be a provincial outpost and began its ascent toward becoming the intellectual heart of the Islamic West.

⚔ Chapter 5 ⚔
Forging a New Dynasty: The Falcon of Quraysh

I. The Umayyad Refugee and the Scars of Al-Andalus

The seizure of Córdoba in 756 was not simply a change of ruler; it was a declaration that the Umayyad spirit—decapitated by the Abbasid sword in the East—had found a new life in the West.

'Abd al-Raḥmān I (later nicknamed Saqr Quraysh, or "The Falcon of Quraysh") was more than a successful general; he was the rightful heir of a fallen caliphate, restoring dignity and legitimate rule to a province teetering on chaos.

Still, legitimacy was a fragile shield in Al-Andalus, a territory long plagued by a history of deep-seated factionalism imported from the East and hardened by isolation.

Arab Settler Feuds: Arab contingents from Syria, Yemen, and Egypt nurtured "jealous rivalries" (Qays-Yaman feuds) that had metastasised into open distrust among the elites.

Berber Resentment: Berber troops, who had carried the initial conquest on their shoulders, "still simmered with resentment" over perceived slights and inequitable land distribution by Arab commanders.

Internal Rebellion: The defeated governor, Yusuf al-Fihri, and his remnants lingered, continually testing the new emir's authority.

External Threats: The Emirate faced pressures from the Christian Kingdom of Asturias in the north and the hostile Abbasid Caliphate in the East, which actively sought to destabilise the Umayyad upstart.

II. Centralisation: The Emir's Pragmatic Hand

ʿAbd al-Raḥmān I understood that raw military victory was insufficient to unite this volatile mosaic. His primary task was to centralise authority without provoking a fatal coalition against him. His strategy was a masterful blend of political pragmatism and calculated reward.

A. Playing the Factions

The emir shrewdly managed the rivalries by playing factions against each other while drawing key leaders into his orbit with titles and land. By preventing any one group from gaining dominance, he ensured that all power flowed back to Córdoba.

B. Creating the Pillars of Power

To enforce this centralised rule, he built a stable, reliable structure independent of the local militias:

1. Professional Standing Army: He created an army large enough to deter widespread rebellion and small enough to remain manageable and loyal to the central government.

2. The Saqāliba Guard (The Palace Slaves): The most crucial component was his personal guard, composed largely of Slavic or European Christian slaves (Saqāliba) who were captured, converted to Islam, and trained as professional soldiers. Their loyalty was absolute, as they owed their entire social and political status entirely to the emir, making them both sword and shield in the treacherous world of palace politics.

Retribution and Administration

Challenges, such as Arab clan leaders withholding tribute or ignoring summonses, were met with "swift retribution." Rebellious towns were surrounded, their leaders executed or exiled, and their lands confiscated and redistributed to loyalists.

Furthermore, ʿAbd al-Raḥmān I began to establish a formal Umayyad administration, reorganising the judiciary under a senior qadi (judge) and implementing a unified legal and tax system.

Infrastructure and Cultural Legacy

To project an image of permanence and prosperity, the emir focused on transforming his capital and consolidating the region's identity.

Reshaping Córdoba

He oversaw vast infrastructural improvements. The city's defences were repaired and extended, markets were reorganised, and key roads leading to the capital were improved, speeding the movement of both troops and essential goods, which fostered economic prosperity and trade.

The Great Mosque as Ideological Statement

The emir's most enduring cultural legacy was the initiation of the Great Mosque of Córdoba (begun in 785 CE). Built on the site of a former Visigothic church, the mosque was more than a place of worship; it was a public and ideological proclamation that the Umayyads were permanently established.

The architecture, which would be expanded by his successors, subtly linked the new regime to the glory of the old Damascus Caliphate, planting the roots of a distinct Andalusi culture.

Conclusion: Setting the Pattern

By the time of his death in 788, ʿAbd al-Raḥmān I had done more than merely survive the chaos and the Abbasid purge. He had successfully transformed Al-Andalus from a fragile, fragmented province into a functioning, independent Emirate with a formidable central authority.

His reign established the fundamental pattern for the next two and a half centuries of Umayyad rule: a sophisticated blend of political pragmatism, decisive military strength, and substantial cultural investment that allowed this western outpost of Islam to flourish into a beacon of knowledge and power in the medieval world.

The forging of the new emirate was not achieved through conquest alone, but through the deliberate act of political imagination. ʿAbd al-Raḥmān I's genius lay not merely in survival or military triumph, but in synthesis — in his ability to bind together Arabs, Berbers, and

Iberian converts into a single, functioning polity. From the ashes of civil strife, he created a state that fused the administrative precision of Damascus with the pragmatic tolerance demanded by Iberian realities. Córdoba became both fortress and forge, shaping a distinctly Andalusian identity that would soon eclipse its eastern counterparts. In its plazas and mosques, the echoes of the desert mingled with the languages of the West, producing a civilisation whose resilience lay in its hybridity. The empire he forged was less a copy of what was lost and more a vision of what could be — a western caliphate tempered by exile, illuminated by learning, and sustained by the iron of necessity.

Aftermath

The emergence of a fluid frontier between Christian and Muslim territories transformed Iberia from a unified political space into a dynamic borderland. Unlike rigid modern frontiers, this was a shifting zone of raids, treaties, marriages, and cultural exchange.

These frontiers became both military laboratories and zones of hybridity. Fortresses rose, alliances shifted, and economies adapted to the constant movement of people and goods. Over time, frontier life would produce new identities—not fully Muslim, not fully Christian, but distinctively Iberian.

Strategically, the frontier slowed Moorish expansion but stabilised their rule. By accepting a de facto limit, rulers could direct energy toward internal governance. For the northern Christian polities, these borders offered breathing space to consolidate their resistance.

The emergence of a fluid frontier between Christian and Muslim territories transformed Iberia from a unified political space into a living organism in constant negotiation with itself. Unlike the fixed lines of modern nation-states, this was a breathing frontier — expanding and contracting with each campaign season, defined as much by diplomacy and marriage as by sword and siege. Raids became ritualised, treaties provisional, and loyalties flexible. Farmers traded across battle lines, mercenaries fought for pay rather than creed, and frontier towns learned that survival required pragmatism more than zeal. What had begun as a military frontier evolved into a social ecosystem where coexistence, however uneasy, became the default condition.

⚔ Chapter 6 ⚔
A Century of Struggle: Consolidation, Crisis, and the Dawn of Culture

The death of the dynastic founder, ʿAbd al-Raḥmān I, in 788 CE, passed the burden of leadership to his son, Hishām I, and, in turn, to his successors.

The rulers of this century inherited a realm united in appearance but deeply fissured beneath the surface. The Umayyad Emirate of Al-Andalus spent the next hundred years battling a three-front war: against internal factionalism, against Christian encroachment from the north, and against the challenge of transforming a military outpost into a sophisticated state.

I. Hishām I (788–796): Piety, Law, Lingering Tensions

Hishām's short reign was characterised by an attempt to anchor the new dynasty in religious legitimacy. Known for his piety and commitment to Islamic law, he actively strengthened Córdoba's religious institutions and sponsored scholars who would later make the city a centre of Maliki jurisprudence. This focus on the Shari'a helped unify the diverse Muslim population under a shared legal code.

However, piety did not solve the political problems. The delicate balance established by his father remained precarious:

Berber Discontent: Berber troops garrisoned on the northern frontiers continued to complain of neglect and mistreatment.

Arab Aristocratic Resistance: The old Arab elites, who had long governed the province, resisted any encroachment on their inherited privileges by the central Cordoban administration.

II. Al-Ḥakam I (796–822): The Test of Central Authority

It was under Hishām's son, al-Ḥakam I, that these simmering tensions erupted into open crisis. Al-Ḥakam was a severe and decisive ruler, whose determination to enforce central control often led to bloody suppression.

The Toledo Revolt (805)

Toledo, the former Visigothic capital, was a long-standing hotbed of autonomy. Its population was highly diverse, comprising Christians, Jews, and the increasingly influential Muwalladūn (converted Christians).

They resented Córdoba's increasing bureaucratic control and, critically, the heavier taxation imposed by the central government.

The revolt in 805 led to the infamous "Day of the Ditch" (or the Massacre of the Ditch).

Al-Ḥakam I's governor lured the city's leading citizens and nobles—many of whom were Muwallad—to a feast, where they were systematically massacred to eliminate the regional opposition.

Suppressing the revolt required a protracted campaign, and Toledo would rise again more than once, symbolising the fierce resistance to Umayyad centralisation.

Internal Purge

Al-Ḥakam I also faced conspiracies within the capital. In 816, a group of religious jurists (who opposed his worldly lifestyle) and disgruntled nobles plotted to overthrow him.

He met this coup d'état with extreme brutality, executing seventy conspirators and establishing a reputation as a merciless enforcer of dynastic security. This era showed that Umayyad survival hinged on a willingness to use ruthless force against both regional and internal opposition.

Abd al-Raḥmān II (822–852): The Zenith of the Emirate

The reign of ʿAbd al-Raḥmān II marked a strategic shift from mere survival to cultural and economic growth. His three decades in power laid the economic and cultural foundation for the later Umayyad Caliphate.

Economic Transformation

The emir encouraged long-distance trade, strengthening connections with North Africa, Egypt, and even the distant, sophisticated courts of the Abbasids in Baghdad. This economic boom was powered by a revolution in agriculture:

Agricultural Innovation: New crops such as sugarcane, cotton, and citrus fruits (like sour oranges) were introduced on a commercial scale.

Irrigation Systems: Extensive irrigation networks were constructed, transforming the fertile Guadalquivir valley into a massive engine of agricultural production.

The Blossoming of Córdoba

Córdoba blossomed into a true political and cultural capital. Artisans produced fine silks, leather goods, and embossed metalwork that were highly prized across Europe and the wider Mediterranean world.

Crucially, ʿAbd al-Raḥmān II made a deliberate effort to import the cultural sophistication of the East:

The Arrival of Ziryab: The arrival of Ziryab (Abū al-Ḥasan ʿAlī ibn Nāfiʿ), a musician, poet, and cultural innovator from Baghdad, revolutionised court life. He introduced refined etiquette, culinary innovations, new fashions, and sophisticated musical styles that fundamentally shaped Andalusi culture and would echo through Spanish history for centuries.

Administrative Modernisation: The emir began to modernise the state bureaucracy (Diwan) by modelling it on the sophisticated Abbasid system, allowing the court to manage the vastly increased revenue from taxes and trade.

Recurring Unrest and the Unshaken Emirate

Despite the cultural achievements, the century was perpetually defined by recurring unrest. The state was constantly tested by the fitna—civil discord:

Social Revolt

Muwallad revolts erupted when these converts, despite adopting Islam, felt excluded from power and privilege by the ruling Arab aristocracy.

Demonstrated a fundamental socio-political division between conqueror and converted.

External Pressure

The Christian kingdoms in the north, especially Asturias, seized on any moment of instability to launch deep raids (ghazawāt) into Muslim lands.

Forced the Umayyads to divert resources and maintain a constant state of military readiness on the frontier.

The emirate endured, but it was not yet unshakable. It remained a realm in the making, its borders contested, its loyalties conditional, and its prosperity dependent on the political and military acuity of its rulers. The struggles of this century—of balancing war, internal politics, and cultural ambition—forged the resilience that Al-Andalus would rely on for the golden age to come.

The Christian kingdoms of the north, particularly Asturias under the early successors of Pelayo, understood that the new emirate was powerful but far from secure. Each rebellion within Al-Andalus, each succession crisis in Córdoba, offered an opening for swift, punishing incursions. These northern expeditions — the *ghazawāt* in reverse — were as many tests of morale as of might.

Small bands of warriors crossed mountain passes, plundered rich valleys, and vanished before a counterattack could form. Their aim was not conquest, but reminder: that the frontier was never still, that vigilance was the price of empire. For the Umayyads, this forced an unending mobilisation of men and money, draining resources that might otherwise have gone to civic building or trade.

Aftermath

The early decades of Muslim rule in Iberia were marked by tension between central authority in Damascus and the realities on the ground. Governors had to balance Arab elites, Berber troops, local Christians, and distant imperial oversight. The result was a series of rebellions and power struggles that exposed the fragility of Moorish control.

Berber resentment simmered beneath the surface. They had provided much of the manpower for the conquest, but often received fewer rewards. Arab elites, meanwhile, jockeyed for dominance, importing old tribal rivalries into Iberia.

These conflicts were crucial: they determined whether Al-Andalus would remain a temporary outpost or develop into a lasting polity. The fact that order was restored—albeit unevenly—laid the groundwork for the rise of a distinctive Andalusi identity, separate from both North Africa and the Middle East.

The turbulence of these formative decades left scars, but it also produced definition. The uneasy coexistence of Arab, Berber, and Iberian elements forced the early rulers of Al-Andalus to improvise forms of governance that neither Damascus nor Kairouan could dictate. Out of rebellion came adaptation: tax reforms to placate converts, land grants to bind soldiers to the soil, and pragmatic alliances with Christian communities to ensure stability. What emerged was not a mere provincial extension of the caliphate but the embryo of a new civilisation — one tempered by conflict, shaped by diversity, and compelled by necessity to find balance.

⚔ Chapter 7 ⚔
The Stones of Power and the Golden Age: Architecture, Infrastructure, and Renaissance

The Umayyad Emirate, having survived a century of internal struggle, was ready to leverage its stability for unprecedented cultural and economic expansion.

This transformation was crystallised in the strategic investment in architecture and infrastructure, turning Al-Andalus from a frontier province into a global centre of sophistication—the prelude to its legendary Golden Age. The centrepiece of this deliberate policy was the Great Mosque of Córdoba (Mezquita).

The Great Mosque: An Architectural Declaration of Sovereignty

When ʿAbd al-Raḥmān I first laid the foundation stones of the Great Mosque of Córdoba in 785 CE, he was making a profound political statement to three constituencies: Defiance to the Abbasids (The East)

By building a monumental congregational mosque, ʿAbd al-Raḥmān I asserted his independence from the Abbasid Caliphate in Baghdad, who were the only other rulers to construct works of such scale. The mosque served as the symbolic, spiritual capital of the independent Umayyad state.

Erasure of the Visigoths (The Past)

The decision to construct the mosque on the very site of the former Visigothic basilica of Saint Vincent was a potent, architectural declaration: the old Christian order was definitively gone, and the new Umayyad dominion was permanent.

This strategic appropriation established a continuity of sacred space, grafting the new power onto the roots of the old.

The Evolution of Style and Synthesis

The initial structure was modest but immediately unique. It incorporated recycled Roman and Visigothic columns (a pragmatic necessity) and introduced the iconic horseshoe arch—a design rooted in the East but perfected in Al-Andalus.

This early synthesis, blending the classical past with nascent Islamic geometric patterns, foreshadowed the rich, unique style that would later define Andalusi art.

The Mosque as Political and Spiritual Anchor

The mosque became the undisputed "beating heart" of Córdoba and the entire state. It functioned not merely as a place of prayer but as the central nexus of civic life:

Education and Law: It was a great madrasa (school), where Maliki jurisprudence was studied and debated.

Governance: Political negotiations and appointments were often conducted under the symbolic authority of its vast halls.

Visual Proof of Rule: Its continuous expansion by successive rulers (Hishām I, ʿAbd al-Raḥmān II, and spectacularly by al-Ḥakam II) served as a visible, physical meter of the dynasty's wealth, piety, and increasing stability.

Strategic Investment in Infrastructure and Defence

Beyond the capital's grand architecture, the Umayyads poured resources into the practical infrastructure necessary to sustain a rich state and secure its contested borders.

The Northern Thughūr (Frontiers)

The northern border, facing the growing threat of the Christian kingdoms (Asturias, León), was heavily militarised. The Umayyads established and strengthened a series of fortified towns, the Upper and Middle Marches (thughūr).

Fortified Hubs: Towns like Medinaceli, Zaragoza, and Tudela became crucial military hubs, housing garrisoned troops and serving as launchpads for punitive raids (ghazawāt) into Christian territory.

Communication Networks: An efficient system of watchtowers sprouted along key roads and mountain passes, using smoke signals by day and fire by night to rapidly transmit news of raids to Córdoba.

The Agricultural Revolution: The Waters of Prosperity

The Umayyads perfected the management of water resources, leading to an agricultural boom that fuelled the state's wealth:

Irrigation Mastery: Existing Roman acequias (irrigation channels) were repaired, and complex new channels (qanats) and water-lifting machines (noriah) were engineered, transforming the arid plains into astonishingly fertile land, particularly in the Guadalquivir valley.

New Cash Crops: This water management allowed the mass cultivation of newly introduced cash crops imported from the East, including sugarcane, rice, cotton, and citrus fruits (notably the bitter orange).

These innovations drastically altered the Andalusi diet, landscape, and export economy.

Economic Flow and the Cultural Renaissance

The security provided by the frontier forts and the wealth generated by the agricultural and commercial activity created the conditions for a profound cultural renaissance.

Commerce and Global Reach

Córdoba's markets grew rich not only from local produce but also from vast long-distance trade networks. The city became a Mediterranean exchange point for:

Luxury Goods from the East: Fine silks from Baghdad, exotic spices from India, and high-quality paper (a technology newly imported from the Islamic world).

Goods from the North: Slaves (Saqāliba) and amber from the Baltic, and metals from Europe.

Attracting the Ahl al-'Ilm (People of Knowledge)

Córdoba's wealth and stability acted as a magnet, attracting the finest minds and hands of the entire Islamic Dar al-Islam, establishing the city as the intellectual rival to Baghdad:

Scholarship: Scholars arrived to establish massive libraries and to copy and comment on rare manuscripts in fields from philosophy to astronomy, saving many classical texts that had been lost elsewhere.

Arts and Poetry: Architects worked with marble and sophisticated mosaics, while poets competed to outdo one another in courtly verses (qasidas), celebrating the Umayyad dynasty and refining the Arabic language.

The Umayyad investment in physical permanence (the Mosque), military security (the Thughūr), and economic systems (Irrigation) ensured that the cultural flourishing of the 9th and 10th centuries—the so-called Golden Age of Al-Andalus—was not a lucky accident, but a deliberate, well-funded result of centralised state policy. The foundations were truly set in stone.

Aftermath

The cultural fusion that emerged in Al-Andalus was neither immediate nor harmonious, but its long-term effects were transformative. Arab elites brought language, religion, and administrative structures; Berber troops brought their own customs and social frameworks; Visigothic and Hispano-Roman populations contributed legal traditions, agricultural practices, and a sophisticated urban culture.

The result was a gradual but profound hybridisation. Arabic became the language of power and scholarship, but Romance dialects persisted in local contexts. Religious minorities — Christians (Mozarabs) and Jews — retained legal autonomy under dhimmi status, paying the jizya tax in exchange for protection. Over time, these communities became essential to Andalusi society, providing translators, merchants, physicians, and bureaucrats.

Architecture and urban planning reflected this synthesis: mosques rose alongside former basilicas; Roman bridges and aqueducts were maintained and expanded; new irrigation systems drew on North African expertise. What emerged was neither purely Islamic nor a continuation of Visigothic Iberia, but something new — Andalus, a Mediterranean crossroads where cultures intermingled on an unprecedented scale.

However, this cultural encounter was not without tension. Conversion to Islam, while not forced, created new social hierarchies.

⚔ Chapter 8 ⚔
Faith and Power: The Social Fabric of Al-Andalus

From the earliest days of the conquest, the Umayyad dynasty's governance was inseparable from its management of a religiously and ethnically mixed society. By the 9th century, this diversity—comprising Muslims (Arab, Berber, and converts), Christians, and Jews—had become the Emirate's defining characteristic and its greatest challenge.

The stability and success of Al-Andalus rested upon the rulers' ability to execute a nuanced policy where religious coexistence, or convivencia, was not merely goodwill, but a fundamental political necessity.

The Structure of Religious Coexistence: The Dhimmi System

In the early centuries of Umayyad rule, the Muslims were the political elite but not the demographic majority. To govern this complex population, the Umayyads utilised the established Islamic tradition of the dhimmi (protected peoples) system.

Rights and Protections

The dhimmi system granted non-Muslims (primarily Christians (Mozarabs) and Jews) essential rights in exchange for acknowledging Muslim political supremacy:

Religious Freedom: They were guaranteed the right to practice their faith, maintain their places of worship (churches and synagogues), and run their own communal affairs (including their own legal courts for internal matters).

Property Rights: They could retain their property, land, and businesses.

A Favourable Comparison: For many Christians and Jews, this arrangement was a marked improvement over the often persecutory and restrictive policies that characterised the final years of the Visigothic Kingdom.

The Price of Protection: Taxes and Subordination

In return for this protection, non-Muslims were required to pay special taxes and accept their subordinate social status:

Jizya: The personal poll tax levied on free non-Muslim males.

Kharāj: The land tax, often paid by both Muslims and non-Muslims, though the dhimmi system generally streamlined the tax burden.

While the taxes were a substantial financial necessity for the state, the non-Muslim population was constantly reminded, overtly or subtly, of their subordinate status.

This included restrictions on building new places of worship, open proselytisation to Muslims, and specific dress codes.

The Internal Dynamics of Muslim Society

The ruling Muslim class was itself a diverse and often fractious mix of ethnicities and social classes, complicating the power structure.

The Three Muslim Strata

1. Arabs: The original conquerors, who held the most legitimate claim to high office and aristocratic status, often based on their tribal origins (Yemenis vs. Syrians).

2. Berbers: The vast majority of the soldiers who carried out the conquest. They often felt marginalised and inadequately rewarded, leading to recurring frontier revolts and a persistent source of internal instability.

3. Muwalladūn (Converts): These were Iberian Christians who converted to Islam. Conversion was often motivated by sincere conviction but was undeniably accelerated by the desire to escape the jizya and gain access to higher positions of influence in administration and the military.

The Problem of the Muwalladūn

The muwalladūn became a powerful and large group, but they were perpetually the source of internal tension (fitna). While they often rose to influential positions, they frequently "rebelled when they felt excluded from the highest offices," particularly by the established Arab aristocracy. Their desire for integration and equal access to power fueled some of the most serious revolts of the 9th century, such as those in Toledo.

The Vital Role of Jewish and Christian Communities

The non-Muslim communities were not simply recipients of Umayyad tolerance; they were active, indispensable components of the Emirate's success.

The Jewish Contribution

Though numerically smaller than the Christians, the Jewish community was vital to the economic and intellectual life of Al-Andalus.

Economic Backbone: Jewish merchants possessed extensive trade networks stretching across the Mediterranean, making them crucial for long-distance commerce and the collection of royal revenue.

Intellectual and Administrative Talent: Jewish scholars served as skilled physicians, translators, and administrators at the Umayyad court. Figures like Hasdai ibn Shaprut, who would later rise to become a diplomatic envoy and court physician to the Caliph ʿAbd al-Raḥmān III, exemplify the height of Jewish influence and integration.

The Mozarabic Community

The Mozarabs (Arabic-speakers who remained Christian) preserved their faith and culture under Islamic rule. They often acted as an intellectual bridge, maintaining knowledge of Latin and contributing skills necessary for the bureaucracy and economy.

Their large numbers, however, made their loyalty conditional, and their occasional insurrections (like those in Córdoba in the mid-9th century, known as the Martyrs of Córdoba) demonstrated the ever-present fault lines of convivencia.

The Legacy of Convivencia

The Umayyads recognised that this delicate balance was the engine of their power and wealth. The success of Al-Andalus was not based on forced assimilation, but on carefully managed diversity.

Cultural Fusion: The mixture of faiths and ethnicities created an unmatched cultural richness. In the major cities, one could hear Latin, Arabic, Hebrew, and Berber spoken in the markets. Churches, synagogues, and mosques often stood within walking distance, fostering a unique blend of architectural and artistic influences.

A Political Balance: The state was perpetually engaged in a social balancing act. The Umayyads' power derived from the efficiency of the dhimmi system to generate revenue and the political necessity of giving all diverse inhabitants a stake in the system.

This environment, though marked by limits and intermittent tension, became one of the enduring legacies of the Andalusi experiment— a sophisticated societal laboratory where faith was simultaneously a source of division and a wellspring of enduring cultural power.

The coexistence of communities in Al-Andalus, though imperfect and often fragile, produced a cultural vitality unmatched in contemporary Europe. In the streets of Córdoba, Toledo, and Seville, scholars debated in multiple tongues, merchants traded goods from three continents, and craftsmen fused artistic traditions into a single, radiant aesthetic.

The Umayyad administration, pragmatic rather than utopian, maintained this equilibrium through careful taxation and legal tolerance — ensuring that coexistence served the stability of the state. Faiths coexisted not because hostility vanished, but because necessity demanded cooperation. Out of this tension arose a civilisation that turned diversity into genius: architecture that blended sacred geometries, music that carried echoes from the desert and the Pyrenees, and philosophy that sought unity in difference. It was a fragile harmony, but one that illuminated the world.

Aftermath

The Abbasid revolution in 750 CE transformed the political landscape of the Islamic world, and Iberia did not escape its shockwaves. The overthrow of the Umayyads in Damascus created both a vacuum of legitimacy and an opportunity. The surviving Umayyad prince, Abd al-Rahman, fleeing westward, would turn that crisis into the birth of a new dynasty.

For Al-Andalus, the Abbasid ascendancy meant the end of direct imperial oversight. Governors who had previously ruled in the name of Damascus now found themselves in an ambiguous position. Loyalties were tested: some embraced Abbasid authority, others clung to Umayyad loyalties or pursued autonomy.

This period of uncertainty allowed local power structures to solidify. Arab and Berber elites, freed from constant interference, began to shape Iberia according to their interests. At the same time, the Abbasids, focused on consolidating their eastern domains, paid little attention to the distant peninsula. This geopolitical neglect paved the way for Abd al-Rahman's dramatic arrival and the creation of an independent emirate, a unique political entity at the westernmost edge of the Islamic world.

⚔ Chapter 9 ⚔
The Crisis of the 9th Century: The Anatomy of Collapse

By the close of the 9th century, the Umayyad Emirate faced a profound existential crisis.

The polished cultural veneer of Córdoba under ʿAbd al-Raḥmān II masked a state where central authority was rapidly dissolving. The carefully constructed social contract—the delicate balance between Arab aristocrats, disgruntled Berbers, powerful Muwalladūn converts, and the tax-paying Mozarab Christians—was shattering.

The resulting multi-front civil strife pushed Al-Andalus to the very brink of disintegration, embodied most dramatically by the rebellion of ʿUmar ibn Ḥafṣūn.

The Roots of Disintegration

The deep cracks that widened into the crisis were both social and political:

The Failure of Social Integration

The system of dhimmi protection and Muwallad conversion, while initially beneficial, eventually created powerful, excluded groups: • Muwallad Resentment: The Iberian converts to Islam (Muwalladūn), while achieving power in local administration and the military, were consistently blocked from the highest offices by the entrenched Arab elite.

They saw themselves as second-class Muslims, and their loyalty was conditional.

Berber Disillusionment: The numerous Berber tribal groups, the backbone of the original conquest army, felt continuously marginalised and mistreated by the dominant Arab governors, fueling their readiness to side with any rebel.

Regional Autonomy: Governors in the frontier thughūr (Marches), such as in Zaragoza and Mérida, operated with increasing independence, creating de facto regional principalities (taifas in miniature) that withheld taxes and military support from Córdoba.

Political Impotence and Fiscal Drain

The endless internal revolts led to a severe fiscal and military drain. The rulers of the late 9th century lacked the consistent force or diplomatic skill to manage this crisis:

Fiscal Crisis: Governors in the provinces often "ruled like independent princes," collecting local taxes but sending only a small "fraction to the central treasury." This choked Córdoba's ability to pay its professional army and fund essential infrastructure.

Asturian Pressure: The Christian kingdoms in the north, particularly the Asturian and Galician raiders, expertly exploited the internal chaos. They tested the thughūr "year after year," forcing the

Umayyads to split their scarce attention and troops between costly internal campaigns and necessary border defence.

The most protracted and dangerous challenge to the Umayyad state was the sprawling rebellion led by 'Umar ibn Ḥafṣūn. His revolt was not just a military campaign; it was a potent political and symbolic challenge to the dynasty's legitimacy.

The Rebel's Genesis and Base

'Umar ibn Ḥafṣūn was a Muwallad from a converted Christian family in the rugged hills near Ronda. His background—born of the land but not of the ruling Arab class—allowed him to embody the grievances of the periphery.

Bobastro: The Symbol of Defiance: He established his nearly impregnable base at Bobastro, a massive, defensible fortress complex carved directly into the mountains of the Sierra Nevada. This location was deliberately "beyond the easy reach of Córdoba's armies," providing him with a secure logistical and symbolic centre.

A Coalition of the Disenchanted: 'Umar's power stemmed from his ability to forge an unlikely coalition of the disaffected: disillusioned Berber tribes, resentful Muwalladūn, and Christians who sought an end to Umayyad taxation and control.

From Bandit to Sovereign

Starting as a local bandit exploiting the Andalusi heartland, 'Umar's operations quickly escalated into a full-scale insurgency:

Guerrilla Tactics: He launched "lightning raids," targeting the Emirate's vital infrastructure, burning granaries, seizing tax convoys, and systematically humiliating Umayyad garrisons.

The Shock of Conversion: In a move that "shocked the emirate" and changed the nature of the rebellion, ʿUmar publicly renounced Islam and returned to Christianity (c. 899 CE). This was a deliberate, calculated political signal.

It instantly secured him direct, material aid from the Christian kingdoms in the north and transformed his rebellion from a domestic Muslim dispute into a religious and political war of liberation in the eyes of the Mozarabs.

For nearly three decades, ʿUmar ibn Ḥafṣūn effectively carved out a sovereign state within the Umayyad borders, symbolising the collapse of the Emirate's authority outside the capital's walls.

The Extent of the Crisis

By the late 9th century, the state was characterised by profound fragmentation:

The Toledo Problem: The fiercely independent city of Toledo repeatedly became a theatre of rebellion, demanding costly and resource-intensive sieges that tied up the best Umayyad forces.

Rise of the Local Magnates: In regions like Badajoz and Seville, powerful local families (often Arab, but acting independently) established their own petty dynasties, effectively turning the "idea of a united Al-Andalus... [into] an aspiration rather than a reality." The state was collapsing into a collection of semi-autonomous territories.

The Umayyad Emirate was in a terminal stage of decline. Survival hinged entirely upon the emergence of a "ruler with the will and vision" to violently reassert central power, a leader prepared to break the cycle of rebellion and fiscal insolvency through a comprehensive mix of military force, shrewd political reform, and unyielding diplomacy. The stage was set for the arrival of this strongman, who would not only save the dynasty but elevate it to its golden zenith.

Aftermath

Abd al-Rahman's journey from hunted fugitive to ruler of Al-Andalus is a narrative of survival, charisma, and political vision. His rise marked a decisive turning point: Al-Andalus would no longer be a provincial outpost of a distant caliphate, but a self-contained Islamic state with its own ambitions.

His ability to unite fractious Arab and Berber factions, secure Córdoba, and establish legitimacy was extraordinary. He drew upon his Umayyad lineage to rally supporters who longed for the stability and prestige of the old dynasty. Yet he also proved pragmatic, forging alliances with local notables and using both diplomacy and force to consolidate his rule.

The establishment of Umayyad leadership in Iberia laid the institutional foundations for centuries of relative stability. Administrative systems were strengthened, taxation regularised, and military power centralised. Al-Andalus, once a peripheral frontier, has now become a political centre in its own right — a rival to both Abbasid Baghdad and the emerging Christian polities in the north.

The aftermath of Abd al-Rahman's ascent was nothing short of transformative. In uniting the fractious mosaic of tribes, faiths, and loyalties, he did more than restore a dynasty—he created a new political organism, distinctly Andalusi in spirit yet proudly Umayyad in heritage. His reign marked the beginning of a confident Western Islam, one that would rival the intellectual and cultural brilliance of Baghdad while rooted in the soil of Iberia. Under his vision, Córdoba began its evolution from provincial stronghold to imperial capital, where administration, art, and faith intertwined.

⚔ Chapter 10 ⚔
The Road to Unity: ʿAbd al-Raḥmān III and the Reassertion of State Power

The existential crisis of the late 9th century demanded a singular, ruthless will to survive. That leader emerged in ʿAbd al-Raḥmān III, who ascended the throne in 912 CE at the precocious age of just twenty-one.

His youth was deceptive; beneath the polished facade of a young ruler lay the steel of a man who understood that compromise with separatist rebels meant a slow, terminal death for the state. His reign of nearly fifty years was defined by a methodical and brutal campaign to re-centralise power and achieve the long-elusive goal of a truly unified Al-Andalus.

The Policy of Absolute Submission

ʿAbd al-Raḥmān III's first act was to abandon the wavering policies of his predecessors. From his first year, he set a clear, uncompromising policy: rebellion would be met not with negotiation or clemency, but with total submission—or annihilation. His method was characterised by speed, discipline, and zero tolerance for continued dissent.

Swift and Relentless Campaigns

The Emir personally led a series of swift and relentless campaigns that moved between provinces with impressive strategic speed. His strategy was to strike at key strongholds before their allies could effectively mobilise or respond, thus isolating rebellious centres.

Reward and Retribution: This policy was enforced with stark clarity: Villages that surrendered quickly were spared and rewarded with favour; those that resisted were stormed, their leaders executed, and their lands confiscated and redistributed to loyalists. This scorched-earth policy quickly drained the political oxygen from local revolts.

Targeting the Periphery: He systematically targeted the great semi-autonomous Arab magnates and Berber sheikhs who had turned their regions into personal fiefdoms, forcing them to either swear absolute allegiance to the central treasury or face ruin.

The Fall of Bobastro

The symbolic heart of the resistance was the mountain fortress of Bobastro, the long-standing base of the Muwallad rebel family, the Ḥafṣūnids.

The Final Defeat: Although the patriarch ʿUmar ibn Ḥafṣūn had died in 917, his sons continued the fight for years. In 928 CE, after a protracted period of attrition, siege, and relentless military pressure, the seemingly impregnable fortress finally fell to Umayyad forces.

A Psychological Victory: The capture of Bobastro was more than just a military triumph; it was a profound psychological victory. It signalled to every aspiring regional magnate—Arab, Berber, or Muwallad—that the era of fragmented rule was definitively over, and that no fortress, however secure, could resist the restored power of Córdoba.

Reasserting Authority on the Frontiers

With the internal threat neutralised, ʿAbd al-Raḥmān III immediately turned his attention to securing and professionalising the northern border, the thughūr, where Christian incursions had long been a drain on resources and a source of national humiliation.

The Chain of Defence

He did not simply defend the frontier; he rebuilt and reinforced it, creating a structured, offensive-capable military buffer zone:

Great Frontier Fortresses: Key fortresses—most notably Zaragoza, Medinaceli, and Gormaz—were either rebuilt or significantly reinforced. These bastions were designed to be not just shelters, but staging grounds for rapid counterattacks and major annual summer campaigns (sa'ifa) against the Christian kingdoms of León and Navarre.

Strategic Purpose: This fortified chain served a dual purpose: it shielded the heartland of Al-Andalus from raids, and, crucially, it allowed the Umayyad government to undertake quick offensive strikes when political or military opportunity arose, keeping the Christian north perpetually on the defensive.

Administrative and Military Reform

To ensure that the restored unity was permanent and not dependent on his personal military presence, ʿAbd al-Raḥmān III systematically dismantled the old, unreliable power structures of the Emirate and replaced them with a cohesive, professionalised bureaucracy and army.

Dismantling the Old Guard

He systematically dismantled the old power structures that had allowed the traditional Arab tribal elites to dominate and politicise provincial rule. These powerful families, who often passed governorships down through their lineage, were replaced with new administrators chosen for their competence and whose loyalty was solely to the Emir himself, thus centralising administrative control.

The Professional Army of Loyalty

The new professional army was completely restructured. Its defining characteristics were loyalty through dependence and ethnic diversity:

Ethnic Diversity: The ranks were deliberately drawn from a diverse mix of ethnic groups: loyal Berber tribesmen (who received better pay and status than before), Arabs, a significant contingent of Saqāliba (Slavic soldiers), and even Christian mercenaries.

Binding by Discipline and Pay: The crucial element was that these soldiers were bound together not by lineage or tribal affiliation, but by pay, discipline, and direct loyalty to the person of ʿAbd al-Raḥmān III.

This army, whose existence depended entirely on the central treasury, was the ultimate guarantor of Umayyad power, immune to the factional rivalries that had crippled previous armies.

By the end of the 920s, the work was complete. Through relentless campaigning and brilliant administrative overhaul, the elusive dream of a unified Al-Andalus had been realised.

The realm was stable, secure, and politically cohesive enough for ʿAbd al-Raḥmān III to contemplate his boldest political move yet—one that would elevate Córdoba from a recovered regional power to the undisputed centre of the Western Islamic world.

Aftermath

The formal establishment of the Emirate of Córdoba transformed Al-Andalus into one of the most sophisticated states in Western Europe. By asserting autonomy from the Abbasids while avoiding an outright claim to the caliphate, the early emirs crafted a delicate balance of political independence and religious orthodoxy.

Córdoba emerged as both capital and symbol. Its central administration coordinated taxation, justice, and infrastructure on a scale unseen in post-Roman Europe. Trade routes linked the city to North Africa, the Middle East, and the Mediterranean. Agricultural innovations — from new irrigation systems to the introduction of crops like citrus and rice — boosted prosperity.

This consolidation brought relative peace and a flourishing of cultural life. Yet challenges remained: regional governors retained significant power, Berber factions still simmered with discontent, and Christian enclaves continued to resist in the north. The emirate's durability would depend on maintaining equilibrium among these competing forces.

The consolidation of the Emirate marked the true birth of Andalusi civilisation — a synthesis of governance, faith, and pragmatism that turned a once-fractured frontier into a functioning state. Córdoba's rise was both practical and symbolic: paved roads and aqueducts revived the echoes of Roman order, while mosques and markets pulsed with the vitality of a new Islamic identity. Scholars and artisans found patronage; merchants carried Andalusi goods and ideas across the Mediterranean world.

⚔ Chapter 11 ⚔
The Dawn of the Caliphate: The Ultimate Declaration of Sovereignty

In the pivotal year of 929 CE, ʿAbd al-Raḥmān III stood at the pinnacle of his consolidated authority. The decades-long Ḥafṣūnid rebellion was crushed, the rebellious regional governors were neutralised, the frontiers were secured, and the treasury was flush with the revenues of a stabilised, unified realm.

With the internal challenge decisively quelled, he made a declaration that was both a strategic masterstroke and a definitive shift in the political landscape of the entire Islamic world: he proclaimed himself Caliph (Arabic: Khalīfah).

The Political Imperative: Claiming the Successorship

The title of Caliph—literally, "Successor to the Prophet Muḥammad"—was the supreme claim to both religious and political leadership over the global Muslim community (Ummah). By adopting the title, ʿAbd al-Raḥmān III was not merely accepting an honorific; he was initiating a direct challenge to all rival claimants and elevating the status of Al-Andalus to a world power.

The Decline of the Abbasids (The East)

For nearly two centuries, the title had been held by the Abbasid Caliphs in Baghdad. However, by the 10th century, the Abbasid Caliphate was a "shadow of its former self." Its vast empire was functionally fractured, with power devolved to ambitious regional governors who ruled autonomously while merely acknowledging the Caliph's spiritual authority.

ʿAbd al-Raḥmān III's declaration was a public rebuke to the dynasty that had overthrown and massacred his Umayyad ancestors, asserting that the spiritual leadership they claimed was now vacant and had passed to the legitimate Umayyad heir in the West.

The Threat of the Fatimids (The South)

A more immediate and potent catalyst was the rise of the Fāṭimid Caliphate in North Africa. This was a Shiʿa Ismaili dynasty that claimed descent from the Prophet's daughter Fāṭimah and asserted spiritual authority over all Muslims.

Establishing their power base in Ifrīqiyah (modern Tunisia), the Fāṭimids were aggressively courting the powerful Berber tribes in the Maghreb, posing a direct, imminent military and ideological threat across the Strait of Gibraltar.

ʿAbd al-Raḥmān III's proclamation was a direct challenge to the Fāṭimids, asserting that Córdoba—not Baghdad, and certainly not the Fāṭimid capital of Mahdia (later Cairo)—was the true Sunni centre of Islamic authority in the West, and the only power capable of defending Islam against Shi'a claims.

The Transformation of Sovereignty

The declaration of the Caliphate was accompanied by a total recalibration of state presentation and internal legitimacy.

The New Regnal Identity

'Abd al-Raḥmān adopted the powerful and authoritative regnal title of al-Nāṣir li-Dīn Allāh—"Defender of the Faith of God."

Public Symbolism: His coinage (dinar and dirham), official documents, and public proclamations immediately carried this new styling.

The Khutba: Most importantly, the khuṭba (the official Friday sermon delivered in mosques) was altered to name him as Caliph, a potent, weekly sign to the faithful of where their ultimate political and religious allegiance must lie.

Consolidating Legitimacy at Home

The move solidified 'Abd al-Raḥmān III's authority with every segment of the population:

For Muslims: The proclamation instantly elevated their realm from a distant, fractious province of a divided ummah to an equal, sovereign seat of power alongside the great, historical courts of the East.

For Non-Muslims: The move confirmed that Córdoba was no longer a dependency but a sovereign state with its own destiny, thus stabilising the dhimmi system under a supreme, unchallenged ruler.

International Diplomacy and Mediterranean Influence

With the title of Caliph, Córdoba instantly became a major player in Mediterranean diplomacy, forcing both Muslim and Christian powers to engage with Al-Andalus on new terms.

Engaging the Christian Powers

The Caliphate of Córdoba began receiving and dispatching high-level diplomatic missions from major European powers:

Byzantium: Ambassadors from Constantinople, the seat of the Byzantine Empire, arrived bearing valuable gifts of silks and gold-leaf manuscripts, recognising the Caliph as an equal sovereign power.

Iberian and Frankish Rulers: Christian rulers from the northern kingdoms of León, Navarre, and even the Frankish kingdoms (Holy Roman Empire) sent envoys seeking trade agreements or, critically, military alliances, a testament to the Caliphate's formidable military strength.

Controlling the Maghreb

In North Africa, the declaration had an immediate impact. Muslim rulers in the Maghreb, caught between the ideological pull of the Fāṭimid expansion to the east and the military-economic influence of Córdoba to the north, were forced to weigh their loyalties carefully. ʿAbd al-Raḥmān III used the Caliphate's legitimacy to support loyal Berber tribes and client states against the Fāṭimids, effectively turning the Maghreb into a crucial sphere of Cordoban influence.

The dawn of the Caliphate in 929 CE was more than a title change; it was a recalibration of the political map. The Umayyad Caliphate in Al-Andalus was now the westernmost, self-declared beacon of Sunni Islam, which ʿAbd al-Raḥmān III intended to make politically stable, militarily formidable, and culturally brilliant—the defining features of the new Golden Age.

The assertion of Caliphal authority projected Córdoba's power far beyond Iberia's shores, transforming the western Mediterranean into a stage for ideological and economic contest. Through shrewd diplomacy and selective military campaigns, ʿAbd al-Raḥmān III extended his reach across the Maghreb, using gold, grain, and prestige as tools of persuasion. Trade routes from the Sahel to the Atlantic were secured under Andalusi influence, feeding Córdoba's prosperity and reinforcing its image as Islam's western capital. The Caliph's emissaries, scholars, and merchants became the instruments of soft power, spreading Andalusi culture as much as its creed.

Aftermath

Religious coexistence in Al-Andalus was complex and constantly negotiated. Muslims, Christians, and Jews shared cities, marketplaces, and, at times, intellectual pursuits. The Islamic legal framework allowed for pluralism, but always within a hierarchy where Muslims occupied the dominant position.

This structure created both opportunities and tensions. Jews and Mozarabs often thrived economically, serving as intermediaries between different communities. Intellectual exchange flourished in multilingual environments, contributing to advances in medicine, philosophy, and science.

However, faith could also become a political fault line. Periodic uprisings by Christian groups, particularly in Córdoba in the 9th century, reflected underlying resentments. Likewise, Islamic orthodoxy sometimes clashed with local practices, producing movements of religious reform or backlash.

Ultimately, the interplay between faith and power shaped Andalusi identity. Religion was not merely a private belief system; it was a structuring principle of society, influencing taxation, law, culture, and geopolitics.

⚔ Chapter 12 ⚔
City of Light: The Splendour of Caliphal Córdoba

Córdoba in the mid-10th century, under the Caliphate established by ʿAbd al-Raḥmān III and perfected by his son al-Ḥakam II, was transformed into a legend—the "City of Light." At its zenith, it may have been home to 400,000 people, making it the largest urban centre in Europe and a formidable rival to the great capitals of the Islamic East, such as Baghdad and Constantinople.

This era represented the ultimate achievement of the Umayyad dynasty, a powerful fusion of political stability, economic dynamism, and intellectual brilliance.

I. Architecture: Symbols of Global Authority

The Caliphate's power was made physically manifest through monumental architectural projects designed to showcase wealth and rival global capitals.

A. The Great Mosque (Mezquita)

The city's skyline was dominated by the vast, gleaming expanse of the Great Mosque. The latest expansions under the Caliphs created an architectural wonder:

The Forest of Arches: The prayer hall featured a near-endless "forest of marble columns" beneath the iconic red-and-white striped, double-tiered arches, a testament to Umayyad architectural innovation and engineering.

The Mihrab: The most significant addition was the Mihrab (prayer niche) and the Macsura (caliphal enclosure), which were inlaid with breathtakingly intricate gold mosaic and Byzantine glass. These materials and techniques, often imported or gifted from Constantinople, were deliberately used to assert the Caliph's equality with the Byzantine Emperor.

B. The Palatial Counterweight: Madīnat al-Zahrā'

Just outside Córdoba, ʿAbd al-Raḥmān III built the massive caliphal palace-city of Madīnat al-Zahrā' ("The Shining City").

A Statement of Power: It was constructed as a spectacular symbol of his newly declared Caliphal power, serving as a counterweight to the grandeur of Baghdad and Constantinople.

Opulence and Administration: The complex featured vast, manicured gardens, serene reflecting pools, and stunning reception halls with gilded ceilings. It functioned as the official seat of government, where ambassadors stood in awe of the Caliph's wealth and where the complex state bureaucracy was headquartered.

II. Economic and Urban Sophistication

Córdoba's opulence was sustained by unprecedented urban planning, infrastructure, and a robust commercial network.

The Functioning City

Unlike many European capitals of the time, Córdoba was a model of urban infrastructure:

Paved Streets: The city boasted paved streets, which ran through its dense, bustling markets, facilitating sanitation and transport.

Water and Hygiene: Aqueducts brought fresh water to public fountains and gardens. Furthermore, public baths numbered in the hundreds, serving both the rich and poor—a level of hygiene and public health utterly unmatched in contemporary Western Europe.

Global Commerce

Córdoba served as the terminus for vast international trade routes. Its markets were rich with goods from three continents: • Asian Luxury: Silk from China and high-quality paper from Samarkand (an innovation brought from the Islamic East).

African and European Commodities: Ivory from Africa and amber from the Baltic.

Local Production: The city also exported its own highly prized manufactures, including fine leather goods and ceramics fired in Andalusi kilns.

III. The Intellectual Beacon

The Caliphate deliberately promoted education and scholarship, establishing Córdoba as one of the world's great intellectual centres.

The Caliphal Library

The caliphal library, significantly expanded by al-Ḥakam II (himself a notable scholar), reportedly held hundreds of thousands of volumes—a collection that "dwarfed the collections of contemporary Europe." This library was the centrepiece of the Caliph's patronage of the arts and sciences.

The Crucible of Knowledge

Scholars gathered in Córdoba from across the Islamic world and beyond:

Translators: Philosophers, physicians, and mathematicians convened to work. Crucially, works of classical antiquity by figures like Aristotle and Galen, which had been lost to much of Europe, were preserved and intensely studied in Arabic and, in time, translated back into Latin by scholars. This intellectual exchange eventually played a key role in the European Renaissance.

IV. The Management of Diversity and Security

The convivencia and the Caliph's military strength were the two critical forces that protected this splendour.

Functional Convivencia

Córdoba was a living laboratory of religious diversity:

Intertwined Communities: Muslims, Christians (Mozarabs), and Jews lived and worked within its walls, their districts distinguished but functionally integrated.

Jewish Influence: Jewish scholars, such as Hasdai ibn Shaprut, rose to become trusted diplomats and court advisors of the Caliph, demonstrating the heights of social mobility available within the system.

The Price of Order

The Caliph understood that this prosperity was fragile and entirely dependent on strong central control:

Security Measures: The roads leading to the frontiers were guarded by a network of fortified towns, ensuring internal stability and the reliable flow of trade and revenue.

Constant Vigilance: The Caliph's professional armies were maintained at the highest level of readiness, prepared to crush any internal dissent or repel the probing attacks from the Christian kingdoms to the north (León and Navarre) that continued to challenge the thughūr every campaigning season.

For a generation, Córdoba shone as the City of Light—a beacon of order, wealth, and learning that offered a stark contrast to the poverty and political fragmentation often found elsewhere in Europe. Its cultural and intellectual flourishing confirmed that the Caliphate of Córdoba was a civilisation at its peak.

The security apparatus of the Caliphate reflected both pragmatism and grandeur. Each fortress, each patrol along the frontier roads, was part of a wider philosophy of governance — that stability was not a gift of fate, but the result of constant discipline. The Caliph's vigilance ensured that merchants travelled without fear, scholars moved freely between cities, and Córdoba's treasury overflowed with the fruits of peace.

Yet this peace was never passive; it was guarded by steel and strategy, by alliances as deftly woven as the silk traded in its markets. The shimmering domes and libraries of Córdoba stood not only as symbols of enlightenment but as monuments to the military precision and administrative genius that made such enlightenment possible.

Aftermath

The rivalries between Berber and Arab factions were not peripheral squabbles but central structural challenges. Berbers had been indispensable to the conquest of Iberia, yet they were often marginalised in the distribution of land and offices. Arab elites, especially those of Syrian origin, dominated the upper echelons of power.

This imbalance led to periodic revolts, particularly in frontier regions where Berber garrisons felt neglected. These uprisings destabilised the emirate, forced military responses, and shaped policies on recruitment and settlement.

More profoundly, these rivalries influenced the cultural and social stratification of Al-Andalus. Arabic became the language of prestige, while Berber languages persisted mainly in rural areas. Over time, many Berbers assimilated linguistically and religiously into the dominant Arab-Islamic culture, but not without leaving a distinct imprint on Iberian military organisation and settlement patterns.

The eventual resolution of these tensions under strong rulers like Abd al-Rahman III did not erase the memory of division. Instead, it became part of the historical consciousness of Al-Andalus, shaping attitudes toward governance and identity for centuries.

✕ Chapter 13 ✕
Blood at the Borders: Warfare and the Frontier Life

The immense splendour and prosperity of Caliphal Córdoba were fundamentally dependent upon the defence of a rugged, dangerous periphery: the {Thughūr}—the northern marchlands.

This frontier, separating Al-Andalus from the aggressively expanding Christian kingdoms, was not a static line but a dynamic, fortified zone of constant military and political tension.

This chapter details the harsh reality of life and death along the border, culminating in the major setback at the Battle of Simancas in 939 CE.

I. The Nature of the Thughūr

The Thughūr was the Caliphate's strategic security zone, stretching across the central and northern Iberian Peninsula.

A Fortified Landscape

Geography and Defence: The zone consisted of "rugged, fortified landscapes"—hills, valleys, and river crossings—where control of strategic heights was paramount. Defence rested on a network of permanent garrisons.

Key Strongholds: Cities like Zaragoza, Medinaceli, and the forward post of Simancas served as the nerve centres. Their walls were continuously reinforced with watchtowers, and their local economies were militarised to support the constant defence, with marketplaces echoing the "clang of armour."

A Way of Life: For the inhabitants, particularly the soldiers and their families, the frontier was a proving ground where the threat of a raid was an inherent part of the "rhythm" of daily life.

The Christian Threat

The Christian realms of León, Navarre, and the increasingly powerful County of Castile viewed the unified Caliphate as a serious threat to their expansion but also as an immense source of wealth.

Political Calculation: A strong Córdoba meant stability but also the risk of being permanently hemmed into the northern mountains. The "lure of rich Andalusi towns" and the strategic imperative of expansion meant the Caliphate was never immune to challenge.

The Aim of Raids: Raids were primarily economic and psychological, aimed at "burning crops, driving off livestock," and seizing resources. They were designed to humiliate the Caliph's forces and disrupt the tax base.

II. The Rhythm of Border Warfare

Border conflict was highly seasonal, dictating the timing and nature of military action.

Summer Campaigns (Sa'ifa)

Summer brought the main campaigning season, when the weather and dry terrain favoured mobility for both Christian and Muslim forces.

Northern Offensives: Christian raiding parties would "slip into Muslim lands," execute their devastation, and rapidly retreat before large forces could gather.

Punitive Expeditions: The Caliph's armies responded with carefully planned punitive expeditions (Sa'ifa). These swift, hard strikes were intended to "punish and deter" by laying waste to Christian territories and seizing captives and booty, thereby asserting the Caliph's military supremacy.

The Shock of Simancas (939 CE)

In 939 CE, the frontier balance suffered a major tilt.

The Coalition: King Ramiro II of León, uniting his forces with those of Navarre and Castile, launched a massive, coordinated offensive that met the Caliphal army, led by ʿAbd al-Raḥmān III himself, at the Battle of Simancas (or the nearby al-Handaq, the Trench).

The Defeat: The Christian coalition, fighting with "stubborn cohesion," broke the heavily structured Muslim lines, inflicting a significant defeat. The Caliph's forces were forced into a disastrous retreat, and the subsequent panic allowed Christian raids to push "deeper than they had in decades."

III. Caliphal Response and the Paradox of Trade

The defeat at Simancas served as a brutal reminder that military might requires constant investment and flexible strategy.

Military and Diplomatic Recalibration

The "shock in Córdoba" led to an immediate, comprehensive response:

Reinforcement: The Caliph poured resources into reinforcing the fortifications of key strongholds and increasing the deployment of elite cavalry units—particularly the Berber and Slavic contingents—to the marchlands.

Strategic Diplomacy: Simultaneously, ʿAbd al-Raḥmān III utilised the "complex chessboard of Iberian politics." He focused on diplomacy, offering truce and generous treaties to certain northern rulers (often Navarre) to isolate others (specifically León or Castile), ensuring that no single grand Christian coalition could threaten the Caliphate again.

War and Commerce Side by Side

Despite the constant bloodshed, a surprising and essential dynamic persisted: trade flowed across the frontiers.

Mutual Necessity: Christian merchants came to Córdoba and other Andalusi centres to sell essential timber, iron, and slaves (often captured in their own internal wars).

Muslim traders carried back valuable goods: silk, refined sugar, and fine ceramics, which were unmatched in Europe.

Interdependence: This paradoxical relationship demonstrated that the frontier was not just a barrier but a porous zone of critical interdependence. War and commerce existed side by side, providing mutual benefits and limiting the severity of prolonged conflict.

The lesson burned into the Caliphate was clear: even under unified rule, the "City of Light" could bleed. The frontier was a testing ground for young commanders—many of whom would rise to shape the Caliphate's future—and a constant drain on resources, but its defence was the ultimate guarantor of Córdoba's glory.

This uneasy coexistence of warfare and trade became one of the defining features of Al-Andalus. Every campaign season that sent armies clashing across the frontier also opened markets once the swords were sheathed. Out of necessity, enemies became business partners, bound by the quiet logic of profit even amid hostility.

Aftermath

The economic transformation of Al-Andalus was one of the most remarkable developments of the early Islamic period in Iberia. What began as a conquered land, fractured and uncertain, rapidly became a Mediterranean economic powerhouse, its prosperity rivalling that of the Abbasid East.

Agriculture was at the heart of this change. The introduction and systematic expansion of irrigation systems—including qanats, norias, and complex canal networks—turned previously marginal lands into fertile zones of intensive cultivation. Crops such as citrus, rice, sugarcane, cotton, and pomegranates enriched the agricultural base and created surpluses that could be traded. These innovations did not erase older Roman and Visigothic techniques; they blended with them, producing a uniquely Andalusi model of agricultural efficiency.

Trade expanded in both scale and reach. Córdoba became a nodal point linking sub-Saharan Africa, the Maghreb, the Middle East, and Western Europe. Goods such as silk, ceramics, leather, metalwork, and agricultural produce flowed through its bustling markets. Muslim, Christian, and Jewish merchants worked side by side, benefiting from a shared commercial culture supported by standardised weights, contracts, and legal protections under Islamic law.

The economic boom funded urban growth, monumental construction (including mosques and fortifications), and patronage of scholars and artisans. It also enabled the emirate to maintain standing armies and centralised administration—key factors in its stability.

Yet prosperity had its fractures. Wealth concentrated in urban elites, often Arab families, while rural Berber settlers and Christian peasants remained at the economic margins. Taxation systems, though efficient, placed heavy burdens on non-Muslims, contributing to social stratification. Economic strength was both the backbone and the potential fault line of Al-Andalus: it fueled cultural brilliance but also sowed inequalities that could be exploited in times of political stress.

⚔ Chapter 14 ⚔
The Holy Road: Arteries of Power and Piety

The Caliphate's security depended on more than just fortress walls; ʿAbd al-Raḥmān III and his successors recognised that power was equally dependent on the arteries that connected Córdoba to the wider world.

The most ambitious infrastructural achievement of the 10th century was the creation of a secure, fortified "Holy Road." This project masterfully blended spiritual duty with political strategy and economic necessity, serving simultaneously as a pilgrimage route and a commercial and military lifeline.

I. Strategic Design and Scope

The Holy Road was conceived as a backbone for the Caliphate, ensuring rapid communication and movement across the disparate regions of Al-Andalus.

The Route and Infrastructure

The Lifeline: The road began in the major port of Algeciras, the main entry point for ships arriving from North Africa (the Maghreb). It then wound north through Córdoba and strategically branched out to the vital northern and eastern provinces, connecting major centres like Toledo, Zaragoza, and the crucial Pyrenean passes.

Safety and Logistics: To guarantee security and smooth travel, the route was lined with two key pieces of infrastructure: • Caravanserais (Fundūqs): Walled inns and rest stops where travellers could find secure lodging, food, prayer spaces, and resupply.

Watchtowers (Atalayas): Square, stone-built military structures placed on strategic heights, often "visible from one to the next," ensuring continuous line-of-sight communication over vast distances.

The Symbolism of the Watchtowers

The watchtowers were essential military posts, but they carried a powerful political message. To see the Caliph's banner flying high above the hills was a constant, visible reminder that "Córdoba's reach extended here," guaranteeing that the Caliphate's authority was not confined merely to the city walls.

II. The Trinity of Function: Faith, Force, and Finance

The true genius of the Holy Road lay in its ability to serve three distinct, yet complementary, state purposes simultaneously.

Spiritual and Religious Duty (The Holy Road)

Facilitating the Hajj: The road made the pilgrimage to Mecca (Hajj) dramatically more accessible to Muslims of Al-Andalus.

Pilgrims could travel in "relative safety under the caliph's protection," their journeys guaranteed by stationed soldiers.

Legitimacy and Piety: Sponsoring the Hajj reinforced the Caliph's image as "a pious ruler concerned for the spiritual duties of his people," further solidifying the religious legitimacy of the Umayyad Caliphate.

Military Strategy and Control (The Road of Force)

Rapid Deployment: The improved road network allowed the Caliph's troops to be moved rapidly along its entire length to meet threats at any point on the frontier (Thughūr). This speed was crucial in suppressing internal revolts or responding to Christian raids.

Centralisation: The ability to project force quickly ensured that local lords were reluctant to challenge central authority, making the road a powerful tool of centralised governance.

Economic Artery (The Road of Profit)

Caravans and Commerce: The road facilitated the swift passage of caravans laden with high-value goods—silks, spices, and manuscripts from the East—into Córdoba's bustling markets.

Revenue Generation: Tax collectors were stationed at key points, efficiently generating revenue that not only funded the road's security and upkeep but also flowed directly into the central treasury, affirming that the road was "a line of profit" in the ledgers of merchants.

III. A Microcosm of Andalusi Society

The waystations and caravanserais lining the Holy Road became "microcosms of Al-Andalus" itself, embodying the cultural mixing that defined the Caliphate.

Cultural Exchange: Here, the blend of faiths and ethnicities was on full display: Muslim scholars debated theology, Christian merchants haggled over bolts of cloth, and Jewish physicians exchanged medical texts with travellers from distant Kairouan or Damascus.

The Flow of Information: The road was a conduit for information and culture. "Stories and news travelled faster than any courier," carried by the mingled tongues of traders, pilgrims, and soldiers, ensuring that Córdoba's influence and culture permeated the provinces.

The project required shrewd diplomacy to secure agreements with local lords, often sealed by gifts, strategic marriages, or the less subtle presence of garrison troops.

The Holy Road ultimately became a lifeline for the Caliphate's economy, armies, and its very identity, proving that power was not only about conquest, but about the connection that bound the realm together like a "thread of gold."

Aftermath

The construction of the Great Mosque was more than a religious act—it was a political statement of permanence and prestige. Begun under Abd al-Rahman I and expanded by his successors, the mosque embodied the self-confidence of a regime that saw itself not as a temporary frontier power but as a new centre of the Islamic world.

Architecturally, the mosque fused Syrian Umayyad aesthetics with local Visigothic and Roman materials. Its iconic double arches, horseshoe vaults, and rhythmic columns became visual symbols of Andalusi identity. The decision to build on the site of the old Visigothic basilica of St. Vincent was deliberate: it asserted continuity and supremacy, transforming a shared sacred space into a statement of Islamic rule.

The mosque's expansion mirrored political consolidation. Each new emir added sections, reflecting both religious devotion and the projection of authority. It became a site not only of prayer but of learning, diplomacy, and governance—a physical manifestation of Córdoba's rise as a capital to rival Baghdad or Damascus.

The Great Mosque also had broader cultural effects. Its grandeur attracted artisans, architects, and scholars. It inspired the construction of mosques and public buildings throughout Al-Andalus, standardising architectural motifs that became uniquely Iberian-Islamic. Over time, it came to symbolise not just faith, but the enduring legacy of the Umayyad dynasty in exile.

⚔ Chapter 15 ⚔
The Last Campaign of Ibn Marwān: Asserting Caliphal Reach

While the Christian frontier demanded constant vigilance, not all dangers to the Caliphate originated across the thughūr.

Some were born within its own borders—localised rebellions rooted in family rivalries, ancient grudges, or the fundamental refusal of regional rulers to submit fully to Córdoba's centralised authority.

The challenge posed by the semi-independent domain of the House of Marwān in the far west forced Caliph al-Ḥakam II to assert that the unification achieved by his father, ʿAbd al-Raḥmān III, was not merely historical, but an active and ongoing reality.

The Legacy of Western Autonomy

The Marwānid domain represented one of the last vestiges of the decentralised, feudal power structure that had plagued the earlier Emirate.

The Muwallad Stronghold

The Founder: The domain was carved out decades earlier by Ibn Marwān al-Jilliqī, a powerful Muwallad (Iberian convert) lord. He had successfully resisted both Emir and Caliph, turning his territory into a semi-independent state.

Geographical Advantage: Based around Badajoz and extending into the rugged hills that abutted the Portuguese frontier, the territory was a patchwork of fortified towns and loyal villages.

The people were bound more to the local House of Marwān than to any distant ruler in Córdoba.

The Loyalty of Words: By the mid-10th century, the Marwānid heirs nominally claimed loyalty to the Caliphate, but this was a "loyalty of words, not deeds." Tribute was irregular, orders from Córdoba were often ignored, and fortresses remained garrisoned by men whose first allegiance was familial.

The Strategic Imperative

In 956 CE, Caliph al-Ḥakam II concluded that this autonomy was an untenable liability. The West was strategically vital for three key reasons:

1. Economic Control: It controlled crucial trade routes to the Atlantic coast.

2. Military Buffer: It formed a necessary buffer against potential incursions from Galicia and Portugal.

3. Political Integrity: Allowing a virtually independent lordship to persist was a dangerous "invitation to trouble" and undermined the principle of central authority.

Al-Ḥakam II's Campaign: Force and Prudence

Al-Ḥakam II approached the campaign against the Marwānids with the methodical precision that defined the Caliphal administration. The goal was not indiscriminate destruction, but overwhelming submission.

The Show of Force

The Caliph assembled a large, well-supplied army designed not to burn the west to the ground, but to make a "show of force so overwhelming that surrender would seem the wiser course."

Methodical Advance: The campaign moved deliberately, fortress by fortress, using siege rather than storming where possible. Each stronghold was encircled, its water supplies cut, and explicit terms offered: submit, pay tribute, and accept a Caliphal governor, and their lands and lives would be spared.

Quick Capitulation: This measured strategy worked for many. Many strongholds capitulated quickly, swayed by both the promise of clemency and the terrifying sight of the Caliph's banners approaching the horizon.

The Siege of Marvão

The campaign culminated in the siege of the most defiant stronghold: the mountaintop citadel of Marvão.

Desperate Resistance: Perched "like a stone crown," Marvão was defended by the direct descendants of Ibn Marwān's household troops, men who knew that their dynastic power would end if the gates fell. They fought with a ferocious desperation.

Siege Warfare Mastery: The Caliph's forces demonstrated the Caliphate's advanced military engineering. The siege tightened for weeks:

- <u>Bombardment</u>: Stone-throwing mangonels battered the walls.
- <u>Sapping</u>: Sappers dug beneath the outer defences.
- <u>Escalation:</u> Wooden siege towers were built to match the height of the battlements, allowing archers to deliver overwhelming volleys into the fortress heart.
- <u>Victory by Attrition:</u> Ultimately, "Hunger and disease did what the walls could not withstand forever."

The Aftermath and Legacy

The fall of Marvão marked the symbolic and actual end of the semi-independent western lordships.

The Merciful Conclusion

Al-Ḥakam II ensured the victory served his long-term goal of stability. When the defenders marched out under a flag of truce, the Caliph "kept his word: no massacre followed."

Absorption of Elites: The defeated leaders were transported to Córdoba, where they were given comfortable, if closely watched, residences. This policy removed them as a regional threat but avoided martyrdom, preventing future vendettas.

Structural Integration: Crucially, their fortresses and domains were immediately absorbed into the Caliphate's military and administrative system, garrisoned by professional troops directly loyal to the central government.

The Renewed Truth of Unity

The campaign achieved more than a simple military victory; it secured a key strategic region and demonstrated the absolute, practical reach of Córdoba's Caliphal power.

The episode underscored a foundational truth for every ruler of Al-Andalus: unity was never a permanent condition. It was a resource that had to be asserted, defended, and perpetually renewed, sometimes through cultural investment, sometimes through diplomacy, and often—as at Marvão—at the point of a sword.

Aftermath

The period following Abd al-Rahman I's consolidation saw a gradual but determined effort by his successors to unify Al-Andalus politically and militarily. The frontier against the Christian north remained volatile, and internal factionalism—Arab vs Berber, tribal vs dynastic—threatened cohesion. The emirs responded with policies that blended military reform, diplomacy, and infrastructural investment.

Border fortresses (ḥuṣūn) were reinforced, and marches (thughūr) were organised into administrative zones to secure the frontier and project power into Christian territories. Roads and supply networks were improved to allow for rapid troop movements. At the same time, diplomatic marriages and treaties were used to neutralise rebellious factions and northern rulers when outright conquest was impractical.

Religious legitimacy was strengthened through the patronage of scholars and the judiciary, ensuring that the emir's authority was sanctified by Islamic law. This fusion of pragmatic governance and ideological consolidation helped transform Al-Andalus from a patchwork of conquests into a more stable, centralised emirate.

Yet unity was never absolute. Rebellions flared periodically, especially in outlying regions where local leaders resented Córdoba's growing control. But compared to the chaotic decades following the conquest, this period represented a decisive step toward political maturity—laying the groundwork for the Caliphate's later grandeur.

Chapter 16
The Threshold of Greatness: Zenith and the Seeds of Decline

By the close of the 10th century, Al-Andalus was at the very summit of its golden age. Under the brilliant reigns of ʿAbd al-Raḥmān III and his son, al-Ḥakam II, the Caliphate of Córdoba became the undisputed jewel of the western Islamic world—a political, intellectual, and economic powerhouse rivalled only by Constantinople and Baghdad.

However, this zenith also marked a dangerous threshold, as the very foundations of centralised power began to shift from the dynastic rulers to an ambitious minister.

The Zenith of Córdoba: A City Unmatched

Córdoba's opulence and sophistication in the mid-10th century set it apart from all other European cities.

A. Urban Splendour and Commerce

Population and Infrastructure: With a population potentially reaching 400,000, Córdoba was a megalopolis. It boasted paved streets lit by oil lamps at night, ensuring safety and functionality.

Economic Powerhouse: The souks were bustling centres of global exchange, where merchants traded luxury goods from across the known world: silks from China, spices from India, amber from the Baltic, and high-quality manufactured goods like fine Cordovan leather.

Public Services: The city's commitment to public health and convenience was unprecedented, evidenced by public baths numbering in the hundreds and aqueducts supplying fresh water to the city.

B. Intellectual Supremacy

The Caliphate's intellectual engine reached its peak under the scholarly al-Ḥakam II, whose patronage made Córdoba the capital of Western learning.

The Caliphal Library: Al-Ḥakam II's private library was legendary, rumoured to contain over 400,000 manuscripts. This collection dwarfed any contemporary European library, attracting scholars from across the Dar al-Islam.

The Transfer of Knowledge: Translators worked tirelessly, rendering Greek philosophy and science (like Aristotle and Galen) into Arabic. Crucially, some of these Arabic texts were subsequently rendered back into Latin, providing a vital intellectual lifeline that would later seed the medieval European intellectual revival.

The Fragility of Personal Rule

Despite its seemingly unassailable strength, the Caliphate's unity rested on highly fragile, personal foundations.

A. The Strength of the Rulers

• ʿAbd al-Raḥmān III had forged unity through a combination of personal charisma, unyielding force of arms, and shrewd administrative overhaul.

• Al-Ḥakam II maintained this stability through his extensive patronage of learning, careful diplomacy, and measured but decisive military campaigns that focused on strategic goals rather than glory.

B. International Standing and Military Might

The Caliphate's power was recognised globally:

Diplomatic Reach: Its ambassadors were received with respect in imperial courts like Baghdad (the Abbasids), Constantinople (the Byzantines), and Rome (the Papacy).

Agricultural Base: Advanced irrigation systems made the Guadalquivir valley an incredibly productive breadbasket, providing the secure revenue base needed to fund the large, professional army.

The Shift of Power: The Rise of Almanzor

The carefully maintained stability shattered upon the death of al-Ḥakam II in 976 CE.

The Void: The crown passed to his young son, Hishām II, a child who was immediately relegated to the role of a figurehead, requiring a powerful guardianship.

The Usurper: Into this political void stepped Abū ʿĀmir Muḥammad ibn Abi ʿĀmir, better known to history by his formidable title, Almanzor (al-Manṣūr bi-llāh – "Victorious by God"). Almanzor was a man of humble birth but extraordinary energy, intelligence, and ruthless ambition.

Triumph and Intoxication

At first, Almanzor appeared to be the perfect protector, leading the Caliphate to its greatest military heights.

Unrelenting Campaigns: He led campaign after campaign (sa'ifa) deep into Christian lands, capturing major cities including Barcelona, Coimbra, and, most famously, the symbolic pilgrimage centre of Santiago de Compostela (997 CE).

Glory and Gold: His victories filled Córdoba's treasury with war booty and reinforced the Caliphate's image as a power beyond challenge.

The Internal Corrosion

Yet, behind the façade of external triumphs, Almanzor was systematically eroding the delicate internal balance of the realm:

Caliph as Figurehead: Almanzor effectively usurped real authority; the young Hishām II was kept isolated and powerless—a caliph only in name.

Factionalism: The traditional, stable power-sharing between Arab, Berber, and Slavic court factions was destroyed. Almanzor stacked the army and administration with Berber mercenaries personally loyal to him, alienating the long-established Arab and Slavic elites. The golden age had not yet dimmed; the Great Mosque still gleamed, and envoys still marvelled. But the Caliphate's fundamental stability had been fatally undermined. The very centralisation of power that had made it so formidable under ʿAbd al-Raḥmān III now made it vulnerable as that power shifted from the legitimate Caliph to his ambitious minister. The unity built over two centuries was slowly, inexorably, beginning to fray.

Aftermath

The proclamation of the Caliphate of Córdoba by Abd al-Rahman III in 929 marked the apex of Andalusi political ambition. By claiming the caliphal title, Abd al-Rahman directly challenged both the Abbasid Caliph in Baghdad and the Fatimid Caliph in North Africa. It was an audacious assertion that Al-Andalus was no longer a provincial backwater but a rival centre of Islamic power.

This move was not merely symbolic. Abd al-Rahman III's reign brought internal stability after decades of rebellion. His military campaigns crushed opponents, his diplomacy balanced Christian kingdoms and Muslim rivals, and his administrative reforms centralised authority more effectively than any of his predecessors. Córdoba, under his rule, became the most populous and sophisticated city in Western Europe, with advanced infrastructure, libraries, hospitals, and markets.

The caliphal title also had profound cultural consequences. Patronage of scholars, poets, philosophers, and scientists flourished. Intellectual life in Córdoba rivalled that of Baghdad, and the city became a beacon that attracted talent from across the Mediterranean.

However, the Caliphate's brilliance contained the seeds of its eventual decline. Centralisation required constant resources and loyalty, both of which would erode in later generations. But for a time, Al-Andalus stood at the very pinnacle of political, economic, and cultural power—a western Caliphate that shaped the destiny of Iberia for centuries to come.

The declaration of the Caliphate also reshaped the political psychology of the peninsula. It gave Al-Andalus a sense of destiny and divine legitimacy unmatched by its neighbours. The Christian kingdoms to the north, though militarily weaker, now faced not just a rival but an empire claiming spiritual as well as temporal supremacy. The ideological tone of the conflict sharpened: wars were now fought not merely for land but for the very definition of faith and civilisation. Abd al-Rahman's assertion of caliphal authority transformed local skirmishes into a civilisational contest that would echo across medieval Europe.

Economically, the Caliphate ushered in an age of prosperity. Trade caravans from Sub-Saharan Africa brought gold and ivory; ships from Alexandria and the Levant arrived with silks, spices, and scholars. The Guadalquivir River, once a simple transport artery, became a lifeline of empire, carrying goods from Córdoba to the Atlantic. Agricultural expansion continued apace — irrigation systems expanded, new crops enriched local markets, and urbanisation drew artisans, merchants, and labourers from every corner of Iberia. Wealth flowed into Córdoba's palaces and endowments, funding public works that stunned travellers from the Christian north.

Yet the empire's reach also demanded constant vigilance. The same prosperity that financed art and architecture also invited envy and rebellion. Frontier governors, enriched by trade and tribute, began to accumulate private armies. Berber contingents stationed in the frontier zones grew restless, demanding greater recognition and spoils. Abd al-Rahman's formidable administration held these ambitions in check, but his successors would find it far harder to contain them. Stability in Al-Andalus was always purchased, and the price was unending control.

Culturally, the Caliphate represented the triumph of synthesis. The Arabic tongue became the language of law and learning, but Latin and Romance dialects persisted, shaping a unique hybrid culture. Jewish scholars translated Greek works into Arabic; Christian scribes copied scientific treatises for northern courts. Architecture, too, reflected this blend — the Great Mosque of Córdoba, with its endless rows of arches, became a metaphor for a civilisation built on the fusion of faiths and forms. The Caliphate's cosmopolitanism was both its glory and its fragility: it relied on tolerance, but also on hierarchy; on shared prosperity, but also on strict order.

Diplomatically, Abd al-Rahman III understood that grandeur required recognition. He sent embassies to Constantinople and the Holy Roman Empire, securing treaties with rulers who regarded Córdoba as a peer. His reign marked one of the few moments when Christian Europe and Islamic Iberia coexisted in uneasy admiration. For a generation, the Iberian Peninsula was not the periphery of Christendom, but the meeting point of worlds — the western edge of a vast, interconnected civilisation stretching from the Atlantic to the Indus.

And yet, beneath the splendour, the empire's contradictions multiplied. The Caliphate's stability depended on the charisma of a single ruler and the delicate balance between Arabs, Berbers, Slavs, and native Iberians. Each group held its own ambitions and resentments. When Abd al-Rahman's descendants inherited the throne, the equilibrium he had built began to wobble. The palace of Madinat al-Zahra, his glittering capital, would one day lie in ruins — a monument to a civilisation that reached perfection only to collapse beneath the weight of its own brilliance.

⚔ Chapter 17 ⚔
The Clash at Tours

The wind that swept down from the Pyrenees carried the smell of distant rain and pine forests, a sharp contrast to the dry winds of the Guadalquivir valley. By the early 730s, the Muslim armies of Al-Andalus were no longer content to consolidate their hold over Iberia. The border was porous, the appetite for spoils immense, and the north beckoned like a half-drawn sword.

For two decades, the expansion had been relentless. After the swift collapse of the Visigothic Kingdom, Muslim commanders crossed into Septimania — the region of what is now southern France — and captured key cities like Narbonne (719), establishing garrisons in territory that had once belonged to the Visigoths but was now a borderland between Christian and Muslim worlds.

Narbonne became a forward base, its harbour a link to Al-Andalus and North Africa. From there, expeditions pushed deeper into Aquitaine, probing the political fractures of the Frankish realms.

The governor of Al-Andalus in this critical period was ʿAbd al-Raḥmān al-Ghāfiqī, a seasoned commander and administrator. Unlike the early conquerors, he was not a man of improvisation but of organisation.

He recognised that raids across the Pyrenees were no longer mere opportunism—they were part of a larger struggle for control over the lucrative trade routes of Gaul and the prestige of extending

Islam's frontier further north. Al-Ghāfiqī assembled a force that blended Arab regulars, Berber cavalry, and Andalusi levies accustomed to frontier warfare.

They were not a single, monolithic army; they were a coalition drawn by promise of booty, duty to the amir, and a shared sense of destiny.

On the other side of the mountains, the political landscape of Gaul was fractured but far from passive. The Merovingian kings were weak, their power wielded by the Mayor of the Palace, Charles Martel — "the Hammer." A man of formidable energy and tactical brilliance, Charles had spent years consolidating his hold over the Frankish nobility, using both diplomacy and military force to bring recalcitrant dukes and counts under his authority. He had already crushed rival factions in Neustria and Burgundy; now his gaze turned south, where the Muslim advance threatened to upset the balance of power.

The trigger came in 732, when ʿAbd al-Raḥmān launched a major expedition into Aquitaine. His target was not Charles, but Duke Odo (Eudes) of Aquitaine, an independent-minded ruler whose lands lay between the Pyrenees and the Loire.

Odo had previously reached uneasy truces with Muslim commanders to keep his duchy intact. But in 732, a decisive raid struck deep into Aquitaine, culminating in the sack of Bordeaux.

Chroniclers describe the city as being overwhelmed with brutal efficiency: the defenders crushed, the bishop slain, the city's wealth seized. Odo's army met the invaders on the banks of the Garonne and was utterly routed.

The news spread like wildfire. Smoke rose from Bordeaux, and refugees streamed north. Odo, his army shattered, had no choice but to appeal to Charles Martel—his rival—to help repel the invaders.

It was a desperate move: the price of Frankish aid would be Aquitaine's political submission. Charles agreed, but on his terms. He mobilised his forces methodically, assembling a disciplined army of Frankish heavy infantry, trained through years of internal warfare and drilled to hold formation under pressure.

Meanwhile, ʿAbd al-Raḥmān pressed north. His army, swollen with loot and captives from Bordeaux, moved in a loose, confident column along the ancient Roman roads. Scouts probed the countryside, reporting weak resistance.

His strategy was clear: move swiftly through Aquitaine, raid the rich churches and settlements of central Gaul, and return south before winter set in. There was no expectation of meeting a united Frankish host on the field; the Franks were seen as divided, slow, and provincial compared to the agile cavalry of Al-Andalus.

Yet as the army crossed the Loire River, the tone began to change. The countryside was emptier than expected. Villages had been evacuated or fortified. Frankish scouts shadowed the flanks. The weather turned colder, the skies greyer. Supplies became harder to procure. The Andalusi troops, accustomed to campaigning in warmer climates, began to feel the weight of the north pressing down upon them.

Charles, meanwhile, selected his battlefield with care. Near the town of Tours, close to the wealthy abbey of Saint-Martin, lay a stretch of gently rolling ground bordered by forest.

Here, he positioned his forces on high ground, blocking the road south. He deployed his infantry in dense, disciplined ranks — what later chroniclers would call a "wall of men."

Unlike the levies of Odo, Charles's men were professionals by the standards of the age: hardened by civil wars, drilled to hold formation under pressure, and motivated by both faith and fear of their leader's iron discipline.

The clash was inevitable. ʿAbd al-Raḥmān, realising too late that he faced not scattered levies but a unified Frankish army, had to decide between retreat and engagement. Retreat would mean abandoning loot, captives, and prestige. Engagement promised glory — or disaster. He chose to fight.

The days leading up to the battle were marked by skirmishes between Frankish scouts and Muslim cavalry. The Andalusi horsemen excelled in hit-and-run tactics, harassing the Frankish flanks and testing their lines.

But Charles refused to be drawn out. He held his position, refusing to chase the raiders into open ground. Each night, the cold intensified. The Andalusi camp grew restless. Supplies dwindled. The loot taken from Bordeaux became both a prize and a burden, slowing movement and tempting indiscipline.

Chroniclers from both sides give us tantalising glimpses of these days. Muslim sources emphasise the confidence of the cavalry and their disdain for the "barbarian" infantry. Frankish sources, written later, highlight Charles's piety and strategic patience.

Between these narratives lies a plausible truth: two armies, vastly different in composition and culture, stared at one another across a bleak autumn landscape, neither fully comprehending the other's strengths.

The stage was set. The armies of two worlds — the mobile, loot-rich Andalusi cavalry and the disciplined Frankish infantry phalanx — would collide in a battle that later generations would elevate far beyond its immediate consequences.

But in the chill of that October, neither side knew they were about to write a legend.

Dawn came pale and bitterly cold. A mist clung to the fields outside Tours, pooling in hollows and veiling the treeline in a shifting grey curtain. For the Frankish infantry, this was familiar terrain and weather; for many of the Andalusi cavalrymen — particularly the Berbers — it was an unwelcome reminder of how far they were from their warm, sun-baked homeland.

ʿAbd al-Raḥmān al-Ghāfiqī rode the line before the first engagement, wrapped in a heavy cloak, his eyes scanning the Frankish position. The enemy had not moved. Charles Martel's forces stood in tight ranks, forming a dense block on the high ground, spears and shields braced.

There were no fluttering banners or grand manoeuvres, just grim, disciplined silence. It was not a style of warfare that inspired fear through spectacle — it promised a grinding, attritional stand.

The Muslim cavalry assembled in looser formation on the lower ground. Arab commanders led the central contingents; Berber cavalry occupied the flanks. The mood was confident, but tinged with impatience. Many had expected Charles to break or retreat before a show of force. Instead, they found themselves facing an opponent who refused to play their game.

Shortly after sunrise, the first wave of probing attacks began. Berber light cavalry rode forward in swift, darting movements, loosing arrows and javelins before retreating. It was a classic tactic, designed to test the enemy's discipline and provoke pursuit. The Frankish infantry did not move. Shields overlapped, ranks held firm, the missiles thudding harmlessly against wood and iron.

'Abd al-Raḥmān observed closely. The Franks were unshaken. He ordered a series of feigned retreats, hoping to lure Charles into a premature charge. The Frankish commander refused to budge. Years of internal warfare had forged in Charles and his men an iron patience. They knew that their strength lay in maintaining their dense formation; once broken, their advantage would vanish.

By midday, it was clear that skirmishing alone would not dislodge the Frankish army. 'Abd al-Raḥmān convened his officers beneath a cluster of trees. The debate was fierce. Some argued for withdrawal — they had riches enough, and the weather grew colder by the hour.

Others, driven by ambition and the desire for a decisive victory, urged a full assault. In the end, pride and necessity carried the day. To retreat now, before defeating the Franks, would be seen as weakness both in Al-Andalus and in Damascus.

The decision was made: a full cavalry charge would be launched against the Frankish centre, supported by waves of horsemen attacking the flanks in rapid succession.

The horns sounded. The cavalry surged forward.

The impact was tremendous. Andalusi horsemen, renowned for their speed and skill, crashed against the Frankish wall with disciplined fury. Lances lowered, horses pounding the frozen earth, they sought to punch holes through the infantry line.

But Charles's men had anchored their position on firm ground, their flanks protected by woodland. The cavalry could not easily outmanoeuvre them. The Frankish ranks absorbed the shock, shields locking, spears thrusting forward. Horses reared; riders were unseated; the line held.

Chroniclers describe the scene as chaotic but resolute: wave after wave of cavalry hurled themselves at the Frankish formation, only to be repelled by the disciplined, almost Roman-style infantry tactics. Unlike previous opponents who had broken under cavalry pressure, these Franks stood like a living fortress. Their heavy armour and long experience in close combat gave them the edge in this kind of grinding melee.

As the day wore on, the battle became a test of endurance. The Andalusi cavalry repeatedly withdrew and regrouped, charging again and again. The Frankish infantry fought shoulder to shoulder, hacking with axes and swords when the enemy closed, thrusting spears when they came at speed. Blood soaked the ground; broken shields and fallen horses littered the field.

'Abd al-Raḥmān personally led one of the decisive charges in the afternoon, aiming to break the Frankish centre through sheer force and leadership. His presence inspired the troops, and for a moment, part of the Frankish line buckled under the pressure.

A few ranks wavered, and the cavalry pushed inward. But Charles Martel moved swiftly, reinforcing the weak point, rallying his men with both shouts and the brutal authority of a seasoned commander. What might have become a breach turned instead into a killing ground, trapping the cavalry in a thicket of spears and blades.

As dusk approached, a critical event occurred that changed the tide. Frankish scouts, possibly acting without direct orders, raided the Andalusi camp, targeting the baggage train laden with loot from Bordeaux. Panic rippled through the rear of the Muslim army. Some of the Berber cavalry, fearing for their share of the spoils or believing a full attack was underway, broke away from the front to protect the camp. The cohesion of the cavalry assault faltered.

'Abd al-Raḥmān tried desperately to restore order, but in the confusion, he was struck down, killed in the melee near the Frankish lines. His death, sudden and unannounced, was catastrophic for command and control.

Without their leader, coordination dissolved. Evening shadows lengthened; exhaustion set in. The cavalry withdrew to their camp under cover of darkness, leaving the field to the Franks, who maintained their disciplined line into the night.

Historical Reflection

The Battle of Tours (or Poitiers, as it is also known) has been wrapped in legend for centuries. Frankish chroniclers, notably the Continuations of Fredegar, cast it as a decisive defence of Christian Europe against Islam, portraying Charles Martel as the saviour of Christendom. Muslim sources treat it with less mythic grandeur, recording it as a significant but not existential defeat — a failed raid rather than a holy war.

Modern historians see the battle as a strategic encounter between two very different military systems. On one side stood the mobile, loot-oriented Andalusi cavalry, whose strength lay in rapid movement and psychological shock.

On the other stood the disciplined Frankish infantry, anchored in terrain, refusing to be lured into open manoeuvre. The Franks chose their ground well, neutralising the cavalry's greatest advantages.

The death of ʿAbd al-Raḥmān was likely the decisive moment. A charismatic and experienced leader, his sudden removal during battle sowed confusion at a critical juncture.

It is also possible that the Andalusi army, burdened by loot and operating far from supply bases, was already near the limits of its operational reach. The raid on the baggage train simply accelerated a disintegration already underway.

As night fell over Tours, the battlefield was strewn with broken lances, abandoned shields, and the bodies of men and horses. Both armies were exhausted.

The Franks had not pursued aggressively; Charles Martel's strategy was never to annihilate, but to repel. In the Muslim camp, commanders argued whether to regroup for another day or withdraw south before the weather worsened.

The next morning would decide the fate of the northern advance.

The battlefield on the morning after the clash was eerily silent. The mist returned, curling low over the fields where the dead lay in tangled heaps — Frankish infantry and Andalusi cavalry alike, their differences erased by death.

Crows circled overhead. Scavengers moved quietly among the wreckage. A few wounded groaned faintly, but the great noise of war had ebbed into the dull hush of aftermath.

Charles Martel's army had held its position through the night. The Franks were exhausted, but they remained disciplined, wary of a renewed assault. Yet when the first scouts crept cautiously toward the Andalusi camp, they found it deserted.

Under the cover of darkness, the Muslim forces had withdrawn southward in good order. There had been no chaotic rout — no frenzied flight — but a deliberate, controlled retreat. For a raiding army operating deep in hostile territory, far from supply lines and winter fast approaching, it was the only rational decision.

ʿAbd al-Raḥmān al-Ghāfiqī's body was found near the place where the fiercest fighting had raged. Wrapped in a simple cloak, he was buried by his remaining officers before they departed. His death left a void that no one on that expedition could fill. Without his leadership, the army lacked a unifying figure to rally around for a renewed attack.

Charles Martel surveyed the field and the abandoned camp with a grim satisfaction. He had not annihilated his enemy, but he had repelled them — and in doing so, achieved what many contemporaries believed impossible. Word spread quickly through Aquitaine and into Frankish lands: the northern advance of the Saracens had been stopped.

Strategic Withdrawal

The Andalusi withdrawal was methodical. They carried their wounded, abandoned heavy plunder they could not transport quickly, and moved south through the passes of the Pyrenees.

For many, the campaign had been profitable despite the outcome: Bordeaux had been sacked; vast wealth had been seized; the Frankish countryside had been raided. The death of their commander and the stalemate at Tours, however, meant that the ultimate objective — decisive dominance north of the Pyrenees — had slipped from their grasp.

In Córdoba, reports of the battle were received with a mixture of regret and pragmatism. The Andalusi governors understood the risks of operating so far from their strongholds.

The logistics of maintaining a permanent presence north of the mountains were daunting. Unlike the Visigothic territories that had fallen quickly in Iberia, the lands of the Franks were divided among many local lords but united under Charles's martial leadership.

Any further northern campaigns would require massive investment of men and resources that the Umayyad governors of Al-Andalus, still consolidating their rule, could ill afford.

The campaign was chalked up as a failed raid, not a catastrophic defeat. Raiding into Gaul would continue sporadically in the years that followed — Narbonne would be held for decades — but the ambition to push decisively beyond the Loire was quietly abandoned.

Frankish Triumph and Legend-Making

In the Frankish world, however, the encounter at Tours took on a different meaning. Charles Martel's victory was not simply tactical — it became symbolic.

Monks and chroniclers, particularly the authors of the Continuations of Fredegar, wrote of Charles as the Hammer who had struck down the advancing tide of Islam. Later Carolingian writers embellished the story further, portraying the battle as a climactic defence of Christendom itself.

This was not mere vanity. The Frankish kingdom was in a process of consolidation, and victories such as Tours helped forge a shared identity among disparate tribes and regions.

By presenting the battle as a decisive turning point, Charles's court strengthened his legitimacy and paved the way for the Carolingian dynasty's later claims to imperial status under Charlemagne. It was a moment that could be shaped into legend — and legends, more than facts, shape nations.

Over the centuries, medieval and early modern writers would elevate Tours to almost mythic status. Poets compared Charles Martel to Constantine, monks declared that he had saved Christendom, and later nationalist histories cast the battle as a civilisational clash between Europe and Islam.

This mythic framing obscured the more nuanced reality: the encounter had been fierce, costly, and strategically significant, but it was neither the beginning nor the end of Muslim ambitions in the west.

A Frontier Redrawn

For Al-Andalus, Tours marked the northern limit of expansion. The Pyrenees became the natural frontier, beyond which lay the fractious but resilient Frankish realms. Muslim forces would continue to raid across the mountains for decades, especially into Septimania and Provence, but these expeditions were aimed at plunder and political pressure, not conquest.

Within Iberia itself, the governors focused on consolidating their rule. The Berber revolts of the 740s loomed on the horizon, revealing tensions within the Muslim army itself.

Arab and Berber soldiers, who had fought side by side at Tours, would soon be at odds over pay, privilege, and the burdens of frontier warfare. The logistical limitations exposed by the campaign in Gaul — long supply lines, harsh weather, uncertain allies — became arguments for focusing resources closer to home.

Yet Tours remained a strategic warning: even the most formidable cavalry could be blunted by disciplined infantry in chosen terrain. The Andalusi commanders would not forget this lesson. Future campaigns focused more on diplomacy, alliances with local lords, and holding key passes rather than sweeping advances northward.

The Long Shadow of Tours

The enduring power of the Battle of Tours lies not merely in its immediate consequences but in its memory. For the Franks, it became a foundational story: the moment their ancestors "saved" Europe. For the Muslims of Al-Andalus, it became a cautionary tale — a reminder that their frontier had limits, and that glory could turn to stalemate far from home.

In truth, both armies had fought to exhaustion; both suffered heavy losses; neither side achieved a clear, crushing victory. But the political afterlives of battles often matter more than the reality of their outcome.

Tours entered the European imagination as a clash of faiths, even though contemporaries on both sides were likely motivated more by power, wealth, and survival than ideology.

Aftermath

The Battle of Tours (732 CE) occupies a mythic place in European and Islamic historiography, far exceeding its immediate tactical consequences. Fought between Frankish forces led by Charles Martel and an expeditionary army under ʿAbd al-Raḥmān al-Ghāfiqī, the clash north of the Pyrenees is often framed as a decisive turning point—a moment when the tide of Islam was "turned back" at the gates of Europe. The reality, however, is more complex and revealing.

Militarily, the engagement was significant but not catastrophic for Al-Andalus. The Muslim army was a raiding force rather than a full-scale invasion, operating deep in hostile territory and overextended logistically. The Franks, by contrast, fought on familiar ground, using heavy infantry formations effectively against Muslim cavalry. The death of ʿAbd al-Raḥmān on the battlefield led to a loss of cohesion, prompting a withdrawal rather than an annihilation. Al-Andalus retained its strength south of the Pyrenees; the frontier shifted but did not collapse.

Strategically, however, Tours marked the limit of rapid Muslim expansion in Western Europe. It demonstrated the logistical challenges of sustaining campaigns so far from Córdoba, especially without secure supply lines or reliable local allies. The Frankish kingdoms, increasingly centralised under the Carolingians, proved to be a formidable barrier. For the next centuries, Muslim military efforts north of the Pyrenees would focus on occasional raids or alliances, not permanent conquest.

Politically, the battle boosted Charles Martel's prestige, laying the groundwork for the Carolingian Empire. Frankish chroniclers, eager to enhance their patron's reputation, framed the victory as a civilizational triumph. Later medieval and modern narratives in Christian Europe elevated Tours into a symbolic "defence of Christendom," projecting backwards a sense of existential confrontation that was not fully articulated at the time.

For Al-Andalus, the aftermath of Tours was marked by strategic recalibration. Attention shifted toward internal consolidation: managing Berber revolts, strengthening control over the Ebro Valley, and securing the northern frontier through the creation of fortified marches. Expansion gave way to defensive entrenchment and political development. Tours did not end Muslim ambitions, but they forced a recognition of geographical and logistical realities that shaped policy for generations.

Culturally, the legacy of Tours became a powerful historical narrative tool for both sides. In Christian Europe, it symbolised divine favour and the resilience of the faith. In Islamic historiography, it was often downplayed or reframed as a setback on the periphery rather than a defining defeat. These differing memories influenced how later centuries interpreted the ongoing frontier wars between North and South.

Ultimately, the Battle of Tours represents less a climactic "end" than a pivot point: the moment when the early, explosive phase of Islamic expansion into Western Europe gave way to a more complex, entrenched frontier dynamic. The focus of Andalusi power turned inward—toward Córdoba, consolidation, and the flowering of an extraordinary civilisation within the Iberian Peninsula.

Epilogue to the Chapter

As winter tightened its grip on the Pyrenean passes, the Andalusi army faded back into Iberia. In Córdoba, the governors regrouped, turning their attention to internal affairs and the defence of their frontier. In the north, Charles Martel's prestige soared. He did not pursue a crusade — such concepts did not yet exist — but he strengthened his hold over Aquitaine, Burgundy, and the Rhineland, laying the foundations for future Carolingian expansion.

The fields around Tours slowly returned to quiet. Farmers came to clear the land, bury the dead, and reclaim what had been lost. For them, the battle was not a legend but a memory of terror, fire, and death. For chroniclers, it was a blank canvas upon which empires could paint their narratives.

Centuries later, historians would debate endlessly whether the battle truly "saved Europe." Some would argue that logistical limits, not Frankish heroism, halted Muslim expansion. Others would claim that the disciplined stand of Charles Martel's infantry genuinely turned the tide. Perhaps both are true. Perhaps neither.

What is certain is that Tours marked a shift in momentum. The Muslim advance reached its furthest northern point and began to consolidate south of the mountains. The Franks, emboldened by their stand, began to see themselves not merely as survivors but as defenders of a civilisation. A frontier had been drawn — not just on the map, but in the minds of two worlds.

⚔ Bonus Chapter ⚔
Between Two Dawns: The Last Council of Toledo

The sky above Toledo was painted in fading gold, the last light of day catching on the Tagus River as it curled below the granite bluffs. From the western gate, riders arrived one by one, their horses lathered and eyes wide, bringing news of villages that had opened their gates to foreign banners, of nobles who had vanished north, of bishops who no longer answered summons. No trumpet had sounded, no grand siege had begun, and yet the ancient Visigothic capital was already half lost.

In the courtyard of the Cathedral precinct, Count Theodomir of the Tagus dismounted slowly, listening to the bells calling Vespers. He was a man of middling years, battle-scarred but not yet bent, descended from one of the old Roman–Gothic senatorial families.

The city around him smelled of smoke, incense, and fear. It was not the sharp fear of a besieged city, but the dull, sickly kind that sets in when a people realise the old order is slipping through their fingers like dry sand.

The council had been called in secret. Only the highest clergy, the remaining nobles of the central plateau, and select civic leaders were to attend. But in Toledo, secrets travelled faster than horsemen.

Lanterns flickered in narrow lanes, and whispered speculations followed Theodomir's footsteps like a cold draft. "Have you heard? Tariq's men are at Talavera." "The Jews are negotiating with the Berbers already." "The Witizans are scheming to open the gates."

Inside the cathedral's chapter house, long used for synods and royal councils, the air was thick with beeswax and tension. A great oak table stood at the centre, scarred by decades of debates and decrees. Around it sat a dozen figures who still pretended, if only for the night, to govern a kingdom.

At the head was Archbishop Sindered, a tall, ascetic man whose eyes carried both spiritual fire and political calculation. To his right sat Duke Oppas, a surviving member of the Witizan faction—one of the noble houses once overthrown by Roderic. His silken robes and measured voice betrayed a man who saw opportunity where others saw ruin. Opposite him, a cluster of Roderic loyalists sat stiff-backed, their faces pale from weeks of devastating news: Guadalete lost, the king's fate uncertain, and towns surrendering without a fight.

Theodomir took his seat in the middle of the table, where he could see both sides. He was neither Witizan nor Roderician by nature; his loyalty was to Toledo itself.

He had ridden south in the early days of panic, expecting to find the Arabs bogged down in attrition. Instead, he found empty fields, deserted watchtowers, and Berber light cavalry sweeping north with terrifying precision.

"Let us begin," Sindered said at last. "Time runs shorter than our patience. Every hour we waste in debate, the enemy moves closer."

Oppas leaned forward. "Then let us stop wasting time pretending we have choices we do not. Tariq ibn Ziyad commands thousands. Musa himself sails to reinforce. The king is dead or fled. What remains of the royal army is scattered. Shall we die on these stones for a throne that no longer exists?"

A murmur rippled around the table. Several nobles avoided each other's eyes.

One of the Roderician loyalists, Count Ebas, slammed his fist down. "You would sell the city to the infidel without a fight? You Witizans have plotted with them from the start!"

Oppa's smile was thin. "And your king brought ruin with his arrogance. Were it not for his usurpation, Musa would have found a united realm. Instead, he found bickering factions. You call me a traitor; I call myself pragmatic. Tariq is not here to exterminate. He wants tribute, order, loyalty. We can keep our lands if we bend the knee."

"Bend the knee to pagans?" Sindered's voice cut sharply through the room. "No. This is a test from God. We are chastised for our sins, but we are not abandoned. Those who remain faithful must preserve what we can—not through compromise, but through flight and renewal."

Theodomir recognised the division as if watching a sword split a log: on one side, those who saw submission as survival; on the other, those who saw flight as salvation. Neither side spoke of actual military resistance. Everyone in the room knew there were too few men, too little unity, and too many feuds for that.

Then, unexpectedly, another voice spoke—a quiet, precise tone from the shadows. "Perhaps… there is a third way."

Heads turned toward the archway. A man dressed not as a noble but in fine wool and a scholar's cap stepped into the light: Yosef ben Ezra, one of the leading figures of Toledo's Jewish community.

His presence at a council of Gothic lords was remarkable, but not unprecedented. Under Visigothic rule, Jews had endured councils that stripped their rights, forced conversions, and expulsions. Yet they remained, integral to the city's economic life.

Sindered stiffened. "You were not summoned."

"No," Yosef replied, "but history has a way of summoning those who survive it." He walked calmly to the table. "I bring news that matters to us all. Tariq has sent envoys to our quarter. They offer protection to the city's inhabitants who open the gates peacefully. They promise respect for property and religion, under the dhimma pact, if tribute is paid. The offer is clear. It will not wait long."

Oppas nodded approvingly. "Even the Jews see what must be done."

Yosef's eyes narrowed slightly. "I see what happens to cities that resist. Mérida fell by negotiation. Écija surrendered. Those who fought were burned or enslaved. We will not fight for a crown that persecuted us. We will survive."

The room crackled with unspoken truths.

Theodomir felt the weight of centuries pressing down. Since the end of Roman rule, Toledo had survived by adapting—Visigoths became Romans in language and law, Christians ruled over Jews, nobles squabbled over thrones—but never before had the city stood before a power so swift and alien. And yet, Tariq's campaign was not one of annihilation. It was something colder, more calculating: a replacement of elites, not of people.

Outside, the bells tolled Compline. The council dragged deep into the night. Plans were argued, alliances hinted at. Some nobles whispered about fleeing to Asturias; others, of sending delegations south with keys to the city.

Theodomir spoke little, listening to both camps. He watched Oppas write the first draft of a message to Tariq. He saw Sindered secretly arrange for relics and church treasures to be sent north under armed escort.

He caught Yosef exchanging quiet nods with one of Tariq's Berber envoys, who stood discreetly at the back—silent, watchful, like a shadow of the new dawn approaching.

As the council splintered into factions, Theodomir stepped outside. The night air was cold. Below, the Tagus reflected the stars. The city was not burning yet. It slept, unaware that its fate was being sealed not by siege engines, but by divided hearts.

The cathedral bells marked the passing hours, but time inside the city no longer moved in measured rhythms. It seemed suspended — stretched thin between two worlds.

As night deepened, lanterns burned low in Toledo's streets. A chill wind rose off the Tagus, winding through cloisters and courtyards like an uninvited herald.

Theodomir lingered in the cloister garden, looking toward the western hills. In the darkness, torchlights flickered faintly — scouts returning from the south, or perhaps the first sign of Tariq's advance. Either way, the city was ringed not by walls alone, but by uncertainty.

From the chapter house, voices carried through the stone corridors. The debate had shifted from moral principles to logistics. Who would escort the treasury north? Which families would flee and which would remain to negotiate? Who would control the gates when the Berbers arrived? The council was no longer about saving a kingdom; it was about dividing its remains before dawn.

He turned as footsteps approached. Yosef ben Ezra emerged from the archway, his scholar's cap slightly askew from the long hours. He studied Theodomir with the analytical calm of a man accustomed to surviving regime changes.

"You are not like the others," Yosef said quietly. "You listen before you speak."

"I have seen enough councils to know words often outrun deeds," Theodomir replied. "Tell me—do you trust Tariq's envoys?"

Yosef hesitated. "Trust? No. But I understand their terms. And I understand power when it moves like a tide. You can swim, or you can drown."

Theodomir nodded slowly. He respected candour. The Jews of Toledo had endured Visigothic decrees that stripped them of property, forced baptisms, and barred them from office.

Yet here was Yosef, poised to ensure his community's survival by negotiating directly with a conqueror his former rulers barely understood. History, Theodomir thought bitterly, had a cruel sense of irony.

They returned to the chapter house together just as Sindered concluded his plan. "The relics and archives will leave at dawn," the Archbishop declared, his voice resonant. "Those who wish to preserve the faith must go north. God will raise a new David in the mountains, and we must prepare the ground."

Oppas stood immediately. "Then go, holy father. I will stay. Someone must speak for the city to Tariq. If I can keep my estates, I will keep the city alive in some form. History will judge who was wiser."

"History," Sindered replied, "will judge who remained faithful."

The fracture was complete. What had begun as one council now became two competing exit strategies: one spiritual, one political. Neither believed arms could defend Toledo.

The Berber envoy finally stepped forward. His presence, until now silent, was like a sudden shift in air pressure. Clad in simple wool, his eyes were sharp, his posture relaxed yet commanding. He spoke in clear, deliberate Latin, honed from years of trade and diplomacy.

"Tariq ibn Ziyad does not wish for unnecessary blood," he said. "He asks for the keys to the city, tribute according to the dhimma, and peace. Those who surrender will keep their property, their laws, and their faith under his protection. Those who flee will not be pursued, but they must take only what they can carry."

His words settled like dust on ancient stones—no threats, no bluster—just certainty.

One by one, the nobles aligned themselves. Some clasped hands with Oppas, preparing letters of submission and tribute. Others knelt for Sindered's blessing before slipping away to pack their families and treasures for the northern road. Toledo, heart of the Visigothic kingdom for two centuries, was being quietly dismembered under candlelight.

Theodomir found himself at the centre of a vortex. His ancestors had governed these lands since the Roman senatorial days. He had fought under Roderic's banners.

He had sworn oaths in the Aula Regia. And now he stood at the edge of a choice that would define not only his fate, but the shape of Iberia for generations.

He closed his eyes briefly. What would resistance accomplish? A brief, doomed stand, followed by slaughter. What would flight achieve? A noble's life in the wilderness, perhaps one day reborn as a legend in some northern redoubt. And what of submission? Survival — perhaps even influence under the new rulers — but at the cost of allegiance to the old order.

The bells struck Matins. The first faint light touched the eastern horizon.

In the final moments before dawn, the council dissolved into action. Sindered departed with a small convoy, relics wrapped in linen, escorted by armed clergy. Oppas and his allies drafted terms of surrender and prepared to meet Tariq's vanguard. Yosef slipped away to his quarter, where runners awaited his signal to open the side gates when the Berbers arrived.

Theodomir climbed the cathedral's bell tower. From this vantage, he could see the entire city: the winding Roman streets, the massive walls, the Tagus looping like a silver ribbon. The city looked eternal. It had seen Romans, Visigoths, heretics, and kings. And yet, in that pale light, it seemed fragile — like a great stone beast breathing its last as a new power approached.

In the distance, dust rose along the southern road. Cavalry. Tariq's advance guard.

Theodomir's decision came not as a heroic epiphany, but as a quiet acceptance. He descended the tower and gave instructions for his household: one part of his family would accompany Sindered north; another would remain with him to negotiate. He would split his legacy as the kingdom itself had split — half in exile, half under new masters. It was not noble, but it was survival.

Historical Reflection

The events of this fictionalised council are inspired by multiple contemporary and later accounts. Chroniclers such as al-Maqqari and the Mozarabic Chronicle hint at internal divisions and negotiated surrenders in Toledo after Guadalete. No dramatic siege is recorded; instead, the city appears to have fallen through a combination of elite defection, negotiated terms, and administrative continuity.

The Jewish role, controversial in later polemics, reflects a strategic calculation rather than treachery: after centuries of persecution under Visigothic law, cooperation with Muslim conquerors offered protection under the dhimma system. Similarly, nobles like Theodomir (historically attested in the Treaty of Orihuela in 713) negotiated survival through treaties that preserved local autonomy in exchange for tribute.

The fall of Toledo, then, was not a single event but a quiet unravelling of a kingdom. No walls were stormed, no grand battles fought within the city. Instead, power shifted in candlelit rooms, under the weight of divided loyalties and pragmatic calculations. The decisions made in those hours set the stage for centuries of coexistence and conflict—between Mozarabs and Muslims, Christians and Jews, conquerors and collaborators.

Epilogue Moment

As dawn fully broke, Theodomir walked toward the Puerta del Sol, where Tariq's cavalry was approaching in disciplined silence. Behind him, bells tolled, and the first households began to wake to a new reality. There would be no battle for Toledo. The city would open its gates, and history would turn quietly on its hinges.

Between two dawns — one fading, one rising — Iberia entered a new age.

Epilogue – The Gathering Storm

By the late 10th century, Córdoba stood at the centre of a world that glittered with confidence. From the minaret of the Great Mosque, the mu'adhdhin's call to prayer drifted across tiled roofs, courtyards shaded by orange trees, and streets where merchants hawked their goods in a dozen languages.

Silk from Damascus, pepper from India, and ivory from Africa passed through its markets. Caliphal messengers rode out in every direction—north to the fortified towns of the thughūr, west to Seville and Badajoz, east to the ports of Almería and Valencia, and south to Algeciras, where ships crossed to North Africa.

It was a city of splendour and order, the jewel of the western Islamic world, the pride of Al-Andalus. Yet history has a way of turning its richest moments into the prelude for upheaval.

When al-Ḥakam II died in 976, his son, Hishām II, was still a boy. In theory, the machinery of the caliphate could continue to run smoothly under regents until he came of age.

In practice, it created an opening that one man would seize with both hands. That man was al-Mansur Ibn Abi ʿAmir—to his allies, the most capable administrator and general the caliphate had ever known; to his enemies, an ambitious usurper who ruled in all but name.

At first, Almanzor appeared to be the saviour of Córdoba's greatness. Year after year, he led dazzling campaigns deep into Christian Iberia. His armies took Barcelona in 985, Coimbra in 987, and in his most audacious strike, they reached Santiago de Compostela in 997, carrying the shrine's great bronze doors back to Córdoba as trophies. To the people, these victories were proof that the caliphate's strength was unbroken.

But the truth was more complex. Almanzor had built an army increasingly dependent on Berber mercenaries whose loyalty was personal, not institutional. Arab and Slavic factions at court found themselves sidelined. The caliph himself became little more than a figurehead—his seal used, his presence required at ceremonies, but his voice absent from real decisions.

In the streets and markets, the changes were subtle. The scholars who had once crowded the caliphal libraries began to see their patronage wane, their stipends delayed.

The careful balance between the sword and the pen—the very foundation of Córdoba's golden age—was shifting decisively toward the sword.

Beyond the city's walls, the Christian kingdoms of León, Navarre, and Castile, though repeatedly humbled by Almanzor's campaigns, were learning from defeat. They rebuilt fortresses in stone rather than wood, trained standing armies, and forged alliances that might one day challenge the unity of Al-Andalus.

And perhaps most dangerously of all, the delicate political equilibrium within the caliphate was eroding. The concentration of power in Almanzor's hands meant that the survival of the system depended on one man's will and one man's fortunes. Should he fall, the rivalries he had suppressed might erupt with renewed force.

For now, the façade still gleamed. Córdoba's markets overflowed, its baths steamed in the cool mornings, and the sound of craftsmen's hammers rang out from workshops producing the finest arms and armour in Iberia. Foreign envoys still bowed before the caliph in public audiences, even if they knew where the real power lay.

But for those who looked closely, the signs were clear: the storm was gathering. The armies that returned from the north brought home not just plunder, but new enemies sworn to revenge. The Berber troops who marched at Almanzor's side were loyal while the pay was good, but their roots were far from the Guadalquivir. And the child-caliph, growing up in the shadow of a man who ruled in his name, would have no experience of power when—if—he came of age.

Al-Andalus had reached its zenith, but it had also begun the slow, almost imperceptible descent into instability. When the storm finally broke, it would not simply threaten the frontiers; it would tear at the heart of the caliphate itself, scattering the unity forged over two and a half centuries.

The golden age was not yet over. But in the marble courtyards of Córdoba, in the bustling markets, and on the dusty roads to the frontiers, the first murmurs of change could already be heard—a whisper of thunder beyond the horizon.

Reference Section – The Iberian Chronicles, Books 1–5

Glossary of Key Terms

Al-Andalus – Name given by Muslims to the Iberian Peninsula during Islamic rule (711–1492).

Berbers – Indigenous North African peoples, many of whom played a key role in the conquest of Iberia.

Caliphate – an Islamic state led by a caliph, regarded as the political and religious successor to the Prophet Muhammad.

Convivencia – Period of relative coexistence between Muslims, Christians, and Jews in medieval Spain.

Dhimmī – Non-Muslim subject (Christian or Jew) living under Muslim rule, granted protection in return for paying the jizya tax.

Emirate – Territory ruled by an emir; in Iberia, the Emirate of Córdoba existed from 756 until it became a caliphate in 929.

Jizya – Tax paid by non-Muslims under Islamic rule in exchange for protection and limited autonomy.

Liber Iudiciorum – Visigothic legal code used in parts of Christian Iberia after the Muslim conquest.

Reconquista – The centuries-long effort by Christian kingdoms to reclaim Iberia from Muslim rule, ending in 1492.

Taifa – Independent Muslim-ruled principality formed after the collapse of the Caliphate of Córdoba in 1031.

—

Chronology of Major Events

- 711 – Muslim forces under Ṭāriq ibn Ziyād cross into Iberia, defeating King Roderic at Guadalete.

- 718/722 – Pelagius leads the Asturian victory at Covadonga, marking the symbolic start of the Reconquista.

- 756 – ʿAbd al-Raḥmān I establishes the Emirate of Córdoba, independent of Abbasid control.

- 929 – ʿAbd al-Raḥmān III proclaims the Caliphate of Córdoba.

- 1031 – Collapse of the Caliphate; rise of the Taifa kingdoms.

- 1085 – Alfonso VI captures Toledo, a key Reconquista milestone.

- 1086 – Almoravids defeat Alfonso VI at Sagrajas.

- 1212 – Christian victory at the Battle of Las Navas de Tolosa breaks Almohad power.

- 1236 – Ferdinand III captures Córdoba.

- 1248 – Ferdinand III takes Seville.

- 1492 – Catholic Monarchs Ferdinand II and Isabella I capture Granada, ending Muslim rule in Iberia.

—

Cast of Historical Figures

Christian Leaders

Pelagius (Pelayo) – Founder of the Kingdom of Asturias, hero of Covadonga.

Alfonso I of Asturias – Expanded Asturian control into Galicia and Cantabria.

Fruela I – Consolidated Asturias' hold on the north.

Alfonso II "the Chaste" – Strengthened ties with the Franks and promoted Santiago de Compostela.

Ferdinand I of León – United Castile and León, expanded Christian lands.

Alfonso VI of León and Castile – Captured Toledo in 1085.

Ferdinand III of Castile and León – Took Córdoba and Seville, a key in the Reconquista's high point.

Isabella I of Castile – Queen who, with Ferdinand II, completed the Reconquista.

Ferdinand II of Aragon – Husband of Isabella I; oversaw Granada's conquest.

Muslim Leaders

Ṭāriq ibn Ziyād – Led the 711 invasion; Gibraltar was named after him.

Mūsā ibn Nusayr – Governor of Ifriqiya, oversaw Iberian conquest.

'Abd al-Raḥmān I – Founded the Emirate of Córdoba.

'Abd al-Raḥmān III – Proclaimed the Caliphate of Córdoba, ushering in its zenith.

Al-Ḥakam II – Scholar-caliph, patron of Córdoba's cultural flowering.

Almanzor – Military leader who led campaigns deep into Christian lands.

Yusuf ibn Tashfin – Almoravid ruler, victor of Sagrajas.

Muhammad I – Founder of the Nasrid dynasty in Granada.

Boabdil – Last ruler of Granada, surrendered in 1492.

Religious Figures

Bishop Oppas – Cleric linked in legend to Pelagius' early campaigns.

Hasdai ibn Shaprut – Jewish diplomat and scholar in ʿAbd al-Raḥmān III's court.

St James the Greater (Santiago) – Patron saint of Spain; his shrine became a major pilgrimage site.

Foreign Allies and Adversaries

Charlemagne – Frankish king; involved in early Iberian campaigns.

Charles Martel – Defeated Muslim forces at Tours in 732.

Pope Urban II – Launched the First Crusade; influenced the Reconquista's religious framing.

www.ingramcontent.com/pod-product-compliance
Lightning Source LLC
Chambersburg PA
CBHW041303240426
43661CB00010B/999